Shaken Faith

Shaken Faith

What You Don't Know (and Need to Know) about
Faith Crises and How They Affect Spiritual Growth

Sanejo I. Leonard

FOREWORD BY
Gary Black Jr.

WIPF & STOCK · Eugene, Oregon

SHAKEN FAITH
What You Don't Know (and Need to Know) about Faith Crises and How They Affect Spiritual Growth

Copyright © 2015 Sanejo I. Leonard. All rights reserved. Except for brief quotations in critical publications or reviews, no part of this book may be reproduced in any manner without prior written permission from the publisher. Write: Permissions. Wipf and Stock Publishers, 199 W. 8th Ave., Suite 3, Eugene, OR 97401.

Wipf & Stock
An Imprint of Wipf and Stock Publishers
199 W. 8th Ave., Suite 3
Eugene, OR 97401

www.wipfandstock.com

ISBN 13: 978-1-62564-941-6

Manufactured in the U.S.A.   04/22/2015

This work is dedicated to the "Thomases" of the world, to the doubters, the seekers, and to those who stubbornly persistent at being formed into the image of Christ despite their faith crises.

"The unexamined life is not worth living"
—Socrates

Contents

Foreword by Gary Black Jr. | ix
Preface | xiii
Acknowledgements | xv

Introduction | 1
    The Nature of Spiritual Growth | 3
    The Nature of this Work | 4
    The Power of Story | 6
    The Scope of this Work | 9

1 Historical Shifts in Theology | 10
    Clashing Theologies | 10
    Modernity, the Age of Enlightenment, and Systematic Theology | 11
    Personal Theology | 14
    Theology and the Postmodern Effect | 16

2 Understanding Faith | 22
    Sandy's Faith | 22
    Faith: What Is It? | 23
    Descriptions of Faith (Responses from Interviews) | 24
    Faith and Belief | 27
    Faith and Trust | 29
    "Right" Faith | 31

3 Faith Crisis Defined | 36
    St. John of the Cross and "Dark Nights" | 36
    Descriptions of Faith Crises (Responses from Interviews) | 37
    The Faith Crisis Reality: Can't Avoid It | 41

Contents

4 Cognitive Dissonance and Faith Crises | 42
　Jacob's Wrestling | 42
　Cognitive Dissonance and the Internal Struggle | 44
　Faith Development Theory | 49
　The Cognitive Dissonance Cycle of the Psalms | 52
　Cognitive Dissonance and Changing Views of God | 53
　"Let Me Get There" | 55

5 Questioning God and Theodicy | 57
　Isabella's Theodicy | 57
　Questions within Faith (Responses from Interviews) | 58
　Theodicy | 60

6 Doubt and Faith Crises | 70
　Christian Reflections on Doubt | 71
　Doubt vs. Unbelief | 77
　Reclaiming Doubt and the Story of Thomas | 78

7 Losing Faith: The Fear and Danger | 84
　Progression of Belief in John 20 | 80
　Peter and Judas' Faith Crisis | 85
　The Fight for Faith | 92

8 Resolution of Faith Crises | 98

9 Understanding Faith Crises in the Church | 101
　Three Stories | 101
　The Church | 102

10 Conclusion: Surviving Faith Crises | 111

Appendix A: Questions Used in Study | 117

Appendix B: Ethnographic Descriptions
　　　　　　of Participants | 119

Appendix C: Additional Tables from Interviews | 121

Bibliography | 135

Subject Index | 139

Author Index | 141

Foreword

THE CONTEMPORARY EVANGELICAL CHURCH is a happy place. Or at least that is what most church leaders want us to believe. The music is peppy, the lighting stirs a mood of excitement, the sermon is encouraging and challenging, and the congregation, most of them, wear their smiles as easily as they do their well-fitting and fashionable clothes.

Is this the slow yet methodical symptom of the prosperity gospel virus making its way through our culture? Like Shakespeare's Queen Gertrude, perhaps we should wonder too if "The Lady doth protest too much, me thinks." Maybe we're a little too happy to actually be so happy. Or perhaps maybe were not so happy at all. Could it be that many of our churches have become and are becoming places where we go to prove to others, if not ourselves, that we really are OK, when in fact we are anything but? Perhaps the church has become a place where we go to assure ourselves, or to be convinced by others of what we only hope is true, right, good, and blessed about our lives, while in reality we don't really know any of this for sure. How many of us attend our church services to "get happy," or look happy under the assumption that we can "fake it until we actually make it"? How much of our worship is feigned? How many of the words of the songs we sing do we actually believe? Are the images conveyed in the lyrics we hear realities in our lives? Few of us want to be troubled with such questions. And so the band plays on. . . .

The real question is not whether we look happy. The real question is whether or not there is ample evidence in our lives that as Christ-followers we are people of enduring joy. Joy is a much more robust reality than simply the feeling of happiness. Happiness, we know, is fleeting. It slips through the fingers like a powdery sand at the first hint of doubt and despair, and therefore tends to be rather cheap but in ample supply. Joy, however, is substantive, hardy, and therefore more costly and rare. Joy is the result of

Foreword

the development of a deep confidence that goodness and loving-kindness lay at the bedrock of our destiny. Such confidence is built on a tried and true relationship with the Good Shepherd. And therein lies the rub. Such a relationship must be tried and *found* true. As King David knew all too well, such confidence is forged not on the mountaintops of success and prosperity, but down in the lonely and desolate valleys where the shadows linger. Happiness knows very little about the suffering of gorges, caves, or even vales, whereas hope and joy's transcendence can be discovered only after enduring the long dark and lonely nights that test the very depths of our souls. Happiness is a vapor. Joy is a rock.

What Dr. Leonard has done for us is to capture the essence of the experiences of those who have escaped the darkened mist of doubt where temporal happiness fades. What she discovers is that many sojourners did not have their faith in the goodness of the Good Shepherd crushed. Instead their faith was tempered and fortified. For it is true, she finds, that doubt and crisis in our walk of faith are not something to be feared or avoided at all cost. Instead our honest embrace of the uncertainties and misgivings of the Christian life is a rich field of soil where God's grace and care can mature our character and knowledge of God and God's ways, in a manner few other means of spiritual maturity can or will accomplish.

As a result, the burning questions she raises to the fore are: What are we to do with the prospect of sincere doubts in our churches? Are doubts and doubters welcome in our congregations? How can our church leaders not only validate but also create a hospitable space for probing difficult questions, non-easily answered problems, and for those who ask them? Are we as "believers" secure enough to be with those who question what to us might seem to be, at the moment at least, assumed if not obvious? Or are we afraid that these doubters will expose our secret addictions to certainty and happiness? Do we really possess the faith we profess or are our claims only a mask that hides a closeted mound of neglected doubt of our own? How are we as the body of Christ to begin fearlessly embracing those drifting in a sea of uncertainty, while maintaining our own compass headings? Can we? Some act as if we shouldn't even try. Others suggest avoidance. Dr. Leonard helps us see that we can and we must fearlessly embrace both our doubts and our doubters.

The church has become good at providing sterile, easy answers. Increasingly these answers are to questions few ask or even consider. The real challenge today is to ask and engage the hard questions that come from the messy nature of our real lives. Dr. Leonard encourages us that we have nothing to fear. The Good Shepherd is there to guide, protect, encourage, enlighten, and comfort. He is with us and we can be with him, as we are, in our confusion, pain, and uncertainty. In living our lives with the Lord as our shepherd, we learn that green fields and still waters are provided along the journey through the dark valleys and the threat of our enemies. Peace, we learn, comes not in the absence of doubt and danger, but despite them, through them. Joy and hope, we come to find out, is not found in the absence of pain, confusion, and doubt, but in the midst of them. For as we come to abide in the dwelling place of the Lord, as we are, doubts and all, we discover that goodness and mercy pursues us, all the days of our lives. This is the overwhelming joy of the Lord, which transcends all our understanding and all our misunderstanding and all our lack of understanding, without needing to provide any specific understanding at all. We need not settle for the whims of happiness. The journey toward joy is worth the risk.

Dr. Leonard helps us to see, from the stories of those who have walked through the valley and come out the other side, that love never fails. We would do well to heed her words. Pastors and church leaders would benefit greatly by rethinking precisely how they can shepherd others who are courageous enough to face the reality of the questions that too few of us dare ask or admit to being troubled over. For who else can we be than who we are right now, and where else can we find the freedom and courage to seek the truth than with the people of God? Leonard encourages us to develop our churches, as well as our individual characters, into the kinds of Christ-like manifestations of honest, open, reflective, agents of hope that catalyze authentic, holistic transformation of our individual and communal lives. We would all do well to pursue her vision, for it is the call of the Good Shepherd, who, leaving the ninety-nine, seeks to comfort the lost, confused, and fearful one.

—Gary Black Jr., PhD

Preface

Elaine's Story

ELAINE,[1] A CARING AND fun-loving person, had a difficult childhood. Though she grew up in church, her home life was traumatic. Elaine never knew her father, and her stepfather abused her for many years until her mother and stepfather finally separated. After making some poor choices as a young adult that led her away from her faith, she came back to God and church in her late twenties, at the point of near exhaustion and contemplating suicide. This reconnecting with God and the church came at a pivotal moment and lasted until additional life experiences in her thirties and forties forced her, once again, to struggle with her faith and church.

What separated Elaine's later time of questioning and doubt from her younger days when she withdrew from the church was that there was no desire to rebel. This later time of questioning for Elaine, now in her forties, was due to a changing perspective of God. As she began to grow and change, she could no longer practically connect the theology that was being taught at her church with what she was coming to understand about God. As she began to wrestle with her beliefs and church doctrine, she found that church was no longer a safe place in which to explore these questions. She withdrew from church and began to study and search for herself who God really was. Her faith was being shaken on a core level, and her church, which she had needed at a crucial time in her life, could no longer accept the place where she was in her faith. Attempts to reach out to her were loaded with subtle and sometimes not so subtle concerns for her "salvation."

---

1. All names and personal details have been replaced with pseudonyms to protect the confidentiality of those who have contributed their narratives to this work. Participants will be referred to their number in the footnotes and a fictitious name in the text.

Preface

For Elaine, the verse in Philippians 2:12 regarding "working out your salvation" became her way of life. She indicates that for the first time in her life she is working out her salvation: reading the Bible, listening to sermons, and reading books; unlike any other point in her life, she is struggling to figure out her faith. Yet, she is still deemed by others as one who is "lost." Those who condemn her journey believe she is working out her salvation in a "wrong" way, as if there is only one correct way to do so.

For Elaine, the struggle is now to find a church where she is free to ask questions and doubt, where people are not compelled to find and give her the right answers or "fix" her. She has often felt as if the church and its leaders have tried to be the source of biblical information, believing that correct theology can be found only through them. She expressed that the "Bible is not that mysterious; God is not trying to hide stuff in the Bible from us." Therefore, her quest is to explore who God is and discover what God means in her life. Rather than depend upon a theology that is framed by others, her mission is to understand God for herself.

Elaine's story epitomizes the journey of faith, marked by faith crises and often misunderstood by the local church. Her faith journey mirrors the journey of others, like her, who have struggled to understand God in atypical methods or patterns not always understood or recognized by others. Essentially shunned by her church and the mainstream church in America, Elaine is struggling to understand what it means to be a follower of Jesus.

Acknowledgments

WHEN I STOP TO think about the many ways our lives are changed, influenced, and helped by others, there is literally not enough space to thank or acknowledge all of the people who have been a contributing factor in my life and have helped me to the place of completing this book. I thank many more people in detail in my dissertation, and will add slightly to that original and thorough list of acknowledgements. Here is my attempt to provide the many thanks that are deserved.

To the people who helped edit and/or guide me on this project: Dr. Debbie Gin and Dr. Gary Black Jr., for their mentoring and guidance on the original dissertation, to Barbara Hayes, who helped to copyedit this work, and special thanks to Natalie Contreras, who worked tirelessly with me on this project and has made me sound better than I could on my own.

To WIPF and STOCK publishers, especially Dave Belcher and Matthew Wimer for their help in bringing this project to completion.

To the many professors and teachers who have influenced my life and helped to shape my education from Vanguard and Azusa Pacific Universities respectively.

To the Kern Family Foundation, Dr. Fred Oaks, and Drs. Robert and Patricia Kern, who have created financial and spiritual support in my education and pastoral leadership.

To Norb and Kathy Kohler, for their continual mentoring, support, and friendship.

To the sixty people who allowed me to interview them and who fearlessly and graciously shared their faith crisis experiences.

To the various churches, pastors, and church members over the years who have helped to shape my faith journey both as a parishioner and pastor, and especially Orange County Worship Center, Desert Reign Assembly of God, and Convergence Church.

Acknowledgments

Lastly, to my family: my late father and sister Sharon, my mom, sisters, brothers, brothers- and sisters-in-law, nieces, and nephews, and extended family of aunts, uncles, and cousins (too many family members to name, but I love and treasure you all), who have provided endless love and have been my constant source of support.

Introduction

I GREW UP IN a Christian home with ten brothers and sisters. Growing up in a larger family is its own narrative, but that is for another time. Between the ages of thirteen and fourteen, I began to experience what John Wesley would describe as a crisis that brings one to salvation.[1] Though I was raised in church and had been "saved" many times at various altar calls, something began to shift within me as I realized my life was not what God wanted it to be, and I was stubbornly refusing to give up the final act of full surrender. The crisis reached a point when, in the summer of 1992, on a missions trip to Chicago with my church youth group, I made the decision to surrender completely to Christ, realizing I wanted to struggle and wrestle no more with the Holy Spirit's call to give my life fully to God.

From that point at the age of fourteen, my crisis moments only increased, as my understanding of God and my faith grew and changed. Life requires growth, change, and adjustments to the harsh realities present, and, like most people, I experienced my own set of losses, grief, and challenges to my faith. Moreover, like some honest Christians who find themselves in the grip of doubt, fear, and a spiral of depression, my first round of extreme loss, at the age of twenty-eight with the death of my father, caused me to question everything: my calling as a pastor, the veracity and stability of my relationships, and the Christian theology and platitudes I had grown up embracing and even using in my prior attempts to comfort others. I found that my self-talk of Christian platitudes and attempts at comforting myself, let alone attempts from others to comfort me, were hollow and at times seemed to be nothing more than veiled attempts to get me to feel better. I did not understand the depths of my pain, even as I tried to rationalize the loss: "I knew this was coming; my Dad was eighty-two when he died. Why is this so hard for me? He's no longer struggling and in pain; why don't I feel

1. Maas and O'Donnell, *Spiritual traditions for the contemporary church*: 311.

better about that? Why can't I shake myself out of this sense of sadness and overwhelming pain? What am I supposed to do? How do I attempt to work and minister to others in the midst of this pain? Am I doing something wrong? Is it my fault this pain and loss hurts so profoundly? Am I not trusting God enough? Am I not 'claiming and believing' his promises enough? Why aren't other people taking this loss as hard as I am? Why don't other people around me understand? Why do they just try to ignore the obvious pain and depression I am in? Why aren't all my previously solid attempts to connect with God enough at this time? Why isn't there anything that is enough to comfort me or bring me a sense of peace?" During grief, there are times when nothing seems to comfort or bring peace. After a while, the only thing that brings a sense of calm is simply the diminishing of the intense pain and sadness, and a type of numb feeling that is void only of the intensity of the moment. Sometimes prayer is calming and comforting, but not always, and not always right away. The Christian promises and platitudes that got me to where I was at the age of twenty-eight no longer "worked." Instead I spiraled into an even deeper quest for faith that was real, not trite or shallow; a journey that would provide real answers, even if those answers hurt. I wanted depth and meaning, not hollow words that did me no good. Similar to Neo's journey in the film *The Matrix*, I needed to take the blue pill in order to see the real world beyond the façade of shallow faith that I had been living before but did not realize.

Even as I write for this work about the passing of my father eight years ago, I am once again thrown into the throes of grief, as I also mourn the loss of the first of my siblings to pass away, my older sister, Sharon. Her death was unexpected and sudden, at least to those of us who lived out of state and did not know that her health was deteriorating, as opposed to the long, slow process of watching my father, who wasted away after a debilitating stroke years prior. My faith is once again being challenged as I wrestle with incomparable and overwhelming pain. The challenge of trying to grieve is at times lonely and overwhelming; our culture, and more particularly, the American Protestant church, has a short attention span with little time or need for ritual. Yet, our Protestant and Evangelical churches seem to allow no space to doubt and experience faith crises, these churches seem also to avoid the excruciating and painful process that is grief.

There is a process that we all must go through, though it is not the same for every person, a process of dealing with our painful experiences and trials, thus, allowing our faith to grow. Our churches need to provide

Introduction

space for grief and space for doubt and crises of faith. Ignoring the internal processes of our faith journey does not help us to "move past" whatever we are experiencing and thus bypass pain, as the pain and struggle will come out in other ways, as most psychologists and psychiatrists tell us. Simply claiming and believing that we are healed from our depression, our doubt, or our grief does not mean that, in fact, we are. Space must be given in our churches, not to fix others, but to help journey with them, allowing them to grow in their struggle and grow in their faith. My goal with this book is this: to help others "normalize" their faith-crisis experiences and thus learn how to navigate through them and to help churches see the need for this difficult part of our faith journey. For whatever reason you are reading this book, I pray that you will help to create or allow this space in your sphere of influence.

The Nature of Spiritual Growth

Our spiritual development can move in predictable growth patterns; yet, our spiritual development is also unpredictable. Similar to our mental and emotional growth, the spiritual life is not visible except when it comes out in our actions and words. The spiritual life, though interwoven into community, is individual, a unique journey with God that we cannot control. As hard as we might try to grow past God and control the process and outcome of our growth, our spiritual growth has to be in partnership with what God is doing in our lives. Paul describes this type of growth in Philippians 2:12–13 where he says that God works in us to "will and to act according to his good purpose." Paul begins this thought with a directive: "Continue to *work out* your salvation, for it is God who works *in you to will* and to act according to *his good purpose*" (italics added). We work outwardly, what we can: the behaviors and lifestyle to which God calls us; but it is God who works in us, who causes and allows growth, and who changes and transforms us. In our surrender and obedience, God moves in us, doing what only God can. The process that God alone is responsible for is a mystery, and one that cannot be completely understood, similar to the account or description of the kingdom of God, in Mark 4, in which Jesus describes the seed that sprouts and grows, though the person who scattered the seed "does not know how" (Mark 4:27, NRSV); the kingdom of God grows not because we cause it to grow, but because we diligently spread the seed; it is God who creates the growth. We diligently present ourselves to God, doing outwardly what we know to do, and God works inside us mysteriously and supernaturally transforming our spiritual life, which then permeates our entire being. While faith crises may seem the opposite of spiritual growth, faith crises are, in fact, an important part of our spiritual formation and development.

The Nature of this Work

I have been observing the process of spiritual growth and faith development, crisis, and spiritual formation for many years—first as a pastor, then as an educator and an academic. The questions regarding how crisis moments affect spirituality, whether doubt has a positive or negative impact, and whether crisis moments are necessary to deepen one's faith have held my attention for most of my life. Through many years of pastoral ministry, I have been routinely involved in the lives of church members and friends encountering crisis moments, and I have observed how these difficult moments affect their Christian faith.

When I entered my doctoral program, the phrase "crisis of faith" was largely unfamiliar to me, though I had heard it used from time to time in various contexts. As I did further research, I came to see that this phrase "faith crisis" is one that has received little study and focus over the years, though it is used in different ranging contexts from a negative loss of faith to a difficult experience that helps one redefine and grow in one's faith. From my own personal experience and from what I had read and studied up to that point in my education, my belief continued to deepen that crises of faith are not only real, but that they are necessary to cause our faith to deepen and grow. A faith that does not experience times of trial and testing, as well as times of doubting, questioning, and/or a wrestling with itself, will produce shallow faith. Without a struggle and internal wrestling to understand what we believe and why, our spiritual root system does not deepen as it should.

We may all agree that in order for our faith to grow, there are some things we must go through in order to deepen our faith and transform our character. *Yet, we seem more reticent to go through experiences like times of doubt, times of questioning, and times of challenges to our faith than we do other forms of trial.* We may look at an event that is thrust upon us, such as a serious illness, the loss of a job, or the loss of a loved one, as a "valid" trial and testing experience rather than faith crises. We may view these events as

Introduction

simply given to us to mature and grow in our faith. However, we may be less likely to explore the internal wrestlings, feelings of doubt, and questions that arise from outside forces that are thrust upon us. The reason may be that we have come to label doubt and questioning of our faith as "unspiritual" or simply a sign of a lack of faith. Doubt is looked upon in Christian theology as reflective of a lack of faith or the opposite of faith. Questions directed to, or about, God have also been frowned upon and seen as harmful to our faith. We may accept the reality of suffering in life that illustrates what Jesus said in Matthew 5:45, "He causes his sun to rise on the evil and the good, and sends rain on the righteous and the unrighteous."[2] Unfortunately, however, we may struggle to allow ourselves and others to doubt and question during those times of pain and suffering.

In an article published in the Association of Religion Data Archives on women survivors of the Rwandan genocide, author David Briggs reflected on the need for time and healing before the women in these types of circumstances could talk about the tragedy, let alone forgive, move on, and heal. According to sociologist Donald Miller, "Forgiveness occurs over a long period of time, years, and even then there is a sense that it's never completed."[3] Though forgiveness is vital to our spiritual health, rushing people into forgiveness before they have processed their pain can be damaging both spiritually and emotionally. However, our response is often to direct others as well as ourselves to forgive quickly and move on. Additionally, what we often do not realize is that painful and difficult experiences become a potential catalyst for a faith crisis. The faith crisis often throws a person into a state of confusion, questioning, and sometimes doubting whether what one has believed about his or her faith is really true.

When tragedy hits us, we have the choice to deal with it head on in our faith, or we have the choice to avoid it. In general, we as humans avoid pain, which is a normal response to pain. Yet, the avoidance of pain also causes us to avoid dealing with pain, and unfortunately the promises of peace, joy, and fullness of life in the Scripture have at times been turned into a marker defining one's spirituality. According to this definition of spirituality, if we are not always experiencing joy, peace, and fullness of life, then we are not living a life of faith and trust.

---

2. NIV.

3. Briggs, "Forgiveness in its own time: How faith communities can help trauma survivors heal," para. 25.

In attempting to address our often-used Christian ways of coping, this study sought to examine whether faith crises are important for spiritual growth, and whether there is an acceptance of faith crises in Evangelical Christianity. I wanted to discover how the church sees those who struggle or wrestle with their faith. What I found were common themes regarding the definition of faith, doubt, and the questioning experience that people had within their faith, the role of understanding in a person's faith development, and the changing paradigm that can result from a faith crisis.

Sometimes ignorance is bliss, and what we do not know is better than attempting to know and have all the answers. However, part of this work argues from a position that it is in our humanity, our being that is made in the image of God, to ask, question, challenge, and to know. Though there are things we cannot know and will not know, the image of burying our heads in the sand like ostriches is actually counter to the way we were made. Our curiosity and endeavor to learn and question are what allow us to innovate, develop electricity, build and fly airplanes, and create medicine and vaccines that keep us alive. Therefore, what we do not know *can* hurt us.

The Power of Story

I love hearing people's stories. Reading biographies and watching them on TV have always been one of my favorite things to do. I am fascinated by people's lives, their journeys, and the paths their lives have taken. When the decision was made to interview people for my dissertation, upon which this book is based, the thought of interacting with so many people and hearing their faith journey was exciting. The original idea for my dissertation was to interact with some people I knew and interview them about their faith journey, to see if I could find some common themes regarding doubt, faith crises, and how individuals processed moments when they questioned their faith. The project grew from there to include multiple levels of acquaintances and to provide opportunities for people I did not know to participate. In some situations, people were recommended by others they thought might be good for the project, and so it snowballed and built momentum as I connected to more people. The end result was that I was able to interact with many different types of people. I was able to reconnect with people I had not talked to or interacted with in many years and I was able to connect with people I knew only by name or association. I heard stories

Introduction

from friends and church members about their narratives and their journeys that I would not have had the opportunity to hear shared any other way.

I utilized three avenues to contact people to be part of my study. The first was through Facebook, which consisted not just of family and friends but also acquaintances, people I had known many years ago, and friends of friends. It was not required that they were ever a Christian, just that they had some connection to and therefore an idea of the Christian faith. I then contacted the people within my church, asking anyone who wanted to participate to contact me. Finally, I contacted a second church to be part of the study. I knew the pastor of this church, but I did not know anyone else in his church. I received a total of sixty participants who were willing to share their faith journeys and experiences.

This study analyzed the lives of these sixty people and the unique and often painful stories that made up their crisis moments. Such depth and poignancy cannot be fully defined and explained in a single project. Since each person's story is unique, I have come to believe that hearing and sharing in someone's journey is one of the most sacred experiences in life. Many of the people who responded had a personal story of crisis or challenge that they had experienced and were more than willing to share their experience. Some of the people I interviewed were sharing their story or aspects of their faith journey in detail for the first time, or articulating it in ways they had never done before. Our biographies were always meant to be shared and in so doing, we find commonality, and others can benefit and learn from our life's journey. In every single story, each person had some tragedy or trial that they shared, even if they did not think it was a difficult experience. Most were able to articulate their faith journey in a way that reflected on their difficult experiences, though a few did not link their difficult experiences to any faith challenge or crisis.

For example, Cassandra, an older woman, who had a pleasant demeanor, had a lifetime of experiences to share, including losing a baby at birth and outliving her husband. Despite these experiences, she could not think of a time in her life, difficult or otherwise, when her faith was challenged. Another person, Sophia, a young wife and mother, had several difficult life experiences. She was in a car accident at a young age that left her mother permanently injured. Similar to Cassandra, she could not think of a time in her life when she really doubted God, God's existence, or God's love in her life. Another person I interviewed, Alden, had grown up in the church, had a confident personality and was successful in his career. Although he had not experienced life-changing or life-altering paradigm shifts of God, he shared that he had experienced some inner turmoil after failing a few courses during college, and that the experience forced him to spend time alone with God and understand who he was in Christ, and he overcame the situation. For Alden, the change he experienced was a different understanding of who he was in Christ, not a change in understanding who Christ was to him.[4]

Others, such as Sandra, who went through an intense time of abuse in her marriage and found herself using drugs, questioned why God would allow her to experience such times of suffering.[5] Andrew questioned an aspect of his theology as he struggled to understand why one of his children struggled with severe depression over a period of time despite Andrew and his wife raising their children in a Christian home.[6] He believed that because he had done all of the right things as a parent, his children should not be struggling in the way that his child was. Lynn, although still quite a young woman, had experienced several years of medical and health issues that were life threatening, and she was at the mercy of her family and church friends to help care for her.[7] During this incredible difficulty, she struggled to understand why all of this was happening to her. Finally, Sally, who lost one of her parents just a year prior to the interview and was dealing with the finality of death, was experiencing a time of grieving that caused doubt over the existence of heaven and whether she would ever see her parent again.[8]

These brief glimpses into some of the stories of the respondents reflect how important our personal narrative is. Fortunately, our current postmodern age has helped to revive an understanding of the importance of narrative. Personal narratives connect people to each other, to life, and to God because the context of a life is conveyed in and through a series of stories that illustrate a person's journey through life. It is no wonder that much of the Bible is written as narrative. Sharing our stories with one another helps us to understand not only our own lives, but it is also one of the ways that we learn and grow; I am so grateful to the participants who allowed me

4. R218, digital recording.
5. R104, digital recording.
6. R129, digital recording.
7. R115, digital recording.
8. R216, digital recording.

Introduction

the privilege of hearing and sharing in their experiences. In sharing these experiences with me and allowing me to use it to study so that I could help others, each of these sixty people showed *how much we want our stories and experiences to matter*. Beyond our pain, our triumphs, our loneliness, and our loss, we want our experiences to live beyond us and make some kind of difference for others. Their stories of tragedy, heartache, loss, pain, doubt, hopelessness, healing, forgiveness, restoration, and hope are what fueled this project; it is their stories that provided me new insight into how faith crisis impacts spiritual formation. Therefore, this interview process was an incredible adventure, and I am forever grateful to those who were willing to share their life stories with me.

The Scope of this Work

I will illustrate in this book that it is important to understand faith crises and how these experiences are more present in our lives than we realize, and that not knowing these concepts can be detrimental to our faith. I will also discuss how cognitive dissonance and theodicy are concepts often seen in faith crises. Finally, I will illustrate how faith crises are present throughout the Bible, from Job to Thomas, and even in some of the lesser known stories involving Jacob, Peter, and Judas.

Much of this work consists of components of narratives from many of the sixty people whom I interviewed, as well as biblical narratives from five different figures who reflect a type of faith crisis. The goal is to show that faith crises are more common than we may at first realize, and that the characteristics that reflect a faith crisis—times of questioning, doubt, cognitive dissonance, and struggling or wrestling with one's faith—are exhibited throughout our lives and the lives of many biblical characters. However, before we begin to discuss faith crises, it is important to see what role theology has had on our faith development over the years and how our definition and understanding of the concept of faith have affected our spiritual development and contributed to faith crises.

Therefore, we begin the work by looking at the past, starting with Aaron's story.

1
Historical Shifts in Theology

Clashing Theologies

Aaron grew up in the church, the same church he had been going to all of his life. He had faithfully and passionately served God most of his life, from the time he started going to church as a child. Aaron is a deep thinker who loves to learn and is passionate about studying the Bible. Though his family did not go to church, he still went faithfully; there, he met and married the woman who would become his wife. As Aaron matured and grew in his understanding of God, he began to question things that his church taught him, things that he did not believe were based in Scripture. After a while, there came to be so many disparate things, from what he understood the Bible said, to what he saw practiced and taught in church, that it caused his old theological paradigm to clash with his new understanding of the Bible. During this time of shifting paradigms, Aaron said his faith foundation seemed to be like "Jell-O,"[1] as if there was no secure and firm foundation. Aaron was coming face-to-face with understanding the different theologies that we all develop (often without realizing it) that shapes our understanding of the Bible. Aaron's developing theology was clashing with his church's theology and it created an internal faith crisis.

These types of theological faith crises are not unusual, and many experience similar faith crises, related either to a specific church theology or a larger theological concept, such as baptism, sanctification, predestination, and others. Unfortunately, a lack of understanding of what theology is and the role it plays in our lives, causes these faith crises to become more difficult than they need to be and can often create rifts in churches and relationships.

1. R125, digital recording.

Historical Shifts in Theology

Modernity, the Age of Enlightenment, and Systematic Theology

Modernity and the Enlightenment

Christian theology has changed over the years, from the first few centuries after Christ's death and resurrection and the establishing of notable doctrines such as the Trinity, to the present day and our discussions of eschatology, God's sovereignty and free will, and sanctification. Christian theology has always been evolving and growing. It took centuries for the early church to decide the canon of the Bible and such theological markers as the Nicene Creed. It then took another twelve hundred years for Martin Luther to call Christians back to "sola scriptura," or hearing the Scriptures only. Reformed theology also found its footing in the sixteenth century as John Calvin developed the TULIP understanding of sanctification (predestination), and it took nearly sixteen hundred years after the Nicene creed for the Pentecostal church to reawaken to the gifts and anointing of the Holy Spirit at Azusa Street in Los Angeles in the early twentieth century.

In addition to the fluidity of theology, two significant changes in history and society helped to shape our current understanding of theology and doctrine. The first was the rise of modernity and the scientific revolution. Modernity, which comprises a period of time from approximately the 1500s to the 1900s, has had a significant impact upon society and the church. The forerunners of modernity, the Renaissance and the Enlightenment, helped to establish modernity as a reaction to Premodernity (the beginning of recorded history to the 1500s or the Enlightenment). Professor and theologian Stanley Grenz refers to the Renaissance as the grandmother of modernity and to the Enlightenment as the mother of modernity.[2] The Enlightenment hailed the emerging role of science as the solution to the world's problems and believed humanity had the power to find these solutions in science. Francis Bacon, for example, believed that "people would look to science as providing the key to happiness."[3] The Enlightenment also elevated reason and logic and a human's ability to use the mind to overcome any problem. With this rise of reason and science and the elevation of humanity, the power and influence of the church was waning.[4]

---

2. Grenz, *A primer on postmodernism*, Kindle location 1151.
3. Ibid., location 1126 of 4319.
4. Ibid., location 1114 of 4319.

Prior to modernity, theologians and theological concepts were the source of intellectual pursuit, and reality was defined as an orderly existence with God at the top, or head of, the order.[5] During premodernity, the western church[6] dictated what was appropriate and right to believe about the world, with all disciplines from science to philosophy being filtered through the lens of theology and church doctrine. The church was also largely in control of what happened in the world, intermingling with governments and countries, setting policy, and determining the fate of much of the world. Needless to say, the church had a significant influence upon Western society. Therefore, when the church, for example, refused to accept that the earth revolved around the sun, despite growing evidence from Galileo and Copernicus, the church began to be regarded by society and intellectuals as obsolete. These rejections of scientific discovery in addition to other intellectual and philosophical advancements by others outside the church, continued to reduce the church's influence upon society. Scientific breakthroughs and rational thought introduced a new way of viewing the world, a worldview that elevated science and reason over theology.[7]

The Rise of Systematic Theology

The second series of events that changed the dynamic of the church was the Protestant Reformation in the 1500s and, consequently, the severe blows to the unity of the central church. The Protestant Reformation, taking place in Germany with Martin Luther, in Switzerland with Huldrych Zwingli, and in France with John Calvin, created new church movements that separated themselves from the church. The Protestant Reformation began in many areas as a protest of the abuses within the church. Yet, what resulted were significant theological differences within these protest movements. Martin Luther became the forerunner for the Lutheran church, and from John Calvin and his theology sprang the Reformed tradition, leading to the development of the Baptist and Presbyterian denominations, as well as many

---

5. Ibid., location 1161 of 4319.

6. The main church that existed at this time was the Catholic Church. Though the Eastern Orthodox Church was also in existence since the time of the East-West/Great Schism in 1054 CE, the Eastern church has played a lesser role in Western society and receives less attention in the history books and in present society as compared to the Catholic church.

7. Ibid., location 1289 of 4319.

Historical Shifts in Theology

others. Additionally, during this time of the Reformation, wars were taking place, often in the name of doctrine and theology. Splits from the church, sometimes tied to political issues and those in authority, were not received lightly. As Stanley Grenz points out:

> In the eyes of many intellectuals, the doctrinal disputes that divided Christians into competing confessional camps lay behind the armed conflicts that had ravaged the continent. Their disgust with confessional wars led these thinkers to question the validity of doctrine itself. Doctrinal commitments, they argued, only serve to divide people.[8]

Therefore, to the modern intellectual, relying upon science and reason to guide him, religion was nothing more than a factious and superstitious belief system that was no longer relevant.

The combination of the loss of power within the central church, the rise of science and elevation of reason, and the various offshoots within Christianity propelled a need for defined basic beliefs within churches. Each new tradition and offshoot of the church needed to establish what they believed about God and the Bible, and why. As society began to emphasize rational thought over supernatural or emotive concepts, it pushed the intellect and logic to the forefront, and in some ways the church followed suit. As a result, the church developed a "system" of theology, or systematic theology that attempted to order our understanding of God and our relationship with God in rational and structured terms.

Systematic theology attempts to define transcendent concepts, such as sanctification, in an orderly fashion, drawing upon Scripture and years of church theology to determine a doctrinal stance. Nearly every current denomination or church has a form of systematic theology, whether or not it is viewed or appreciated as such. Some congregational theology is simply a list of beliefs or doctrines that are central to that church and thus, become the rudder for that organization. Unfortunately, the initial intent to develop a system of guiding and clear beliefs to organize a faith system has become a spiritual type of straightjacket in many situations. According to Justo Gonzalez in his *Story of Christianity*:

> Theologians in the seventeenth and eighteenth centuries zealously defended the teachings of the great figures [Luther, Calvin, Loyola] of the sixteenth, but without the fresh creativity of that earlier generation. Their style became increasingly rigid, cold, and academic.

---

8. Ibid., location 1208 of 4319.

Their goal was no longer to be entirely open to the Word of God, but rather *to uphold and clarify what others had said before them.* (italics added)[9]

González goes on to say that "Reformed, Lutheran, and Catholic alike developed orthodoxies to which one had to adhere strictly or be counted out of the fold of the faithful."[10] The Reformation of the church that launched new passion and zeal for reading the Bible on an individual level and the counter-Reformation in the Catholic Church that allowed the church to "clean up" some of the abuses within and call people back to a type of "pure" Christian ethos eventually morphed into dogmatic and rigid orthodoxy. Unfortunately, as humans, we are always guilty of venerating individuals beyond what we should, and the church is no less guilty of such veneration. This exaltation of church leaders has led to the deification of their words and ideas; thus, church theology has been viewed in many situations on the same level as Scripture. The famous church leaders over the past two thousand years, from Augustine to Luther, from Teresa of Avila to John Calvin (insert any historical church or modern church leader of any movement or denomination: John Wesley, Ignatius of Loyola, George Fox, Aimee Semple McPherson, etc.), have contributed important theological concepts that help us better understand God and our relationship with God. Doctrinal ideas and beliefs that reflect a mutually-agreed-upon standard of theology can also help to unite a community of believers. However, without realizing it, we can take those teachings and create doctrine that becomes the *only* lens through which we interpret God and the Bible. The doctrine and teachings of leaders in the church often become the starting point for our way of understanding God, rather than one way of understanding God. In an attempt to provide a theological foundation, the doctrine becomes the only standard upon which we build our theological framework.

Personal Theology

Theology, though not a simple concept, simply means the study of God, and it encompasses a person's religious belief system. Dallas Willard described theology as "a way of thinking about and understanding—or

---

9. González, *The Reformation to the Present Day*, 133.
10. Ibid.

Historical Shifts in Theology

misunderstanding—God."[11] What Willard has alluded to here is the reality that our theology is a limited lens through which we view God, based upon what we know or have experienced about God. Though a person's theology may not be "systematic" or even in agreement with his church or denomination, each person has his own belief about God that is based upon his study or understanding of God. Willard also reflects that it is possible to "misunderstand" God through our theology. As fallen human beings, our perspective is limited to begin with. As Paul said in 1 Corinthians 13, "we see in a mirror, dimly"[12] or, as the King James Version says, we "see through a glass, darkly." Paul goes on to say, "Now I know in part; but then shall I know even as also I am known."[13] We do not have a perfect framework from which to understand all aspects of life, let alone God. Therefore, all theology will be faulty in some way, mainly in its limitation to understand, and then describe the fullness of God.

Therefore, though one of the purposes behind systematic theology and a structured understanding of God is avoiding heresy and false doctrines that could lead people astray, it can also restrict a person's ability to understand God from his or her own experience. This ordered and structured understanding of God, the church, and the Bible often leave no room for ambiguity and unresolved questions, and can discourage a person's own unique faith and faith experience. A disorderly interruption of our belief system can cause crisis and chaos within a systematized approach to knowledge, which is something that Aaron experienced. As he was growing in his own understanding and study of the Bible, his understanding struggled to accept what he had previously been taught. Systematic theology is meant to organize our understanding of God, and a disorganized questioning of such beliefs can be seen as a move outside of the realm of order and structure. This was the case for Aaron, whose story was mentioned at the start of this chapter; his struggle to accept his church's "systematic" theology on a variety of issues became the impetus for him not only leaving that church, but prior to that, was the source of much angst as he struggled to reconcile what he believed Scripture to say with what his church was telling him it said. As he struggled to reconcile what he believed, the freedom to disagree with the church while remaining connected to the church, became part of the struggle.

11. Willard, *The Spirit of the Disciplines*, 14; italics added.
12. 1 Cor 13:12, NRSV.
13. KJV.

Avoiding heresy and false beliefs about God is important, and the church has a long history of using defined and mutually agreed upon beliefs such as theology as a way to help people understand God and as a means to form a person's system of belief. However, the emphasis has been on "right" belief (what the church determines is the right belief) and this belief encourages the person to behave in certain ways according to this systemized understanding of God. Systematic theology, though helpful and necessary at times, becomes the foundation of presumption from which modern doctrine has been taught. While such structured beliefs can be said of any organization that has a group of people, what makes systematic theology unique is that the theology itself is its power to affect how individuals behave. Systematic theology also emphasizes, perhaps without knowing it, the importance of "belief" (mental agreement) primarily as the definitive marker of one's salvation.[14] "Right belief" comes from the Latin, *orthodoxy*, and has become, in many situations, the hallmark of one's Christianity. Without said orthodoxy, one is in danger of losing his or her salvation and straying from the Christian faith.

This does not mean, however, that we do away with doctrine, theology, or even systems of theology. It does mean that we need to approach our doctrine with more humility, recognizing that we "do not know what we do not know," or, we do not realize what we do not know.[15] Unfortunately, the focus in systematic theology and doctrine seems to be on finding and holding to the "right" doctrine and theology, rather than allowing theology to become personal, evolving, and growing.

Theology and the Postmodern Effect

Where modernity and systematical theology have had some negative effects upon faith development, postmodernity may provide a beneficial impact that rectifies some of the extremes within modernity. Postmodernity, similar to all other movements and cultural shifts throughout history, has both negative and positive results, largely because each historical movement is

---

14. This concept of right belief will be discussed in more detail in the next chapter in the discussion of faith and how we define faith.

15. The Johari Window, developed in the 1950s by Joseph Luff and Harry Ingram, illustrates the extent to which what we do not know is hidden from us and that only through asking questions and reflection can we know what we do not know. Armstrong, "Revisiting the Johari Window," 10–12.

a reaction to an extreme movement that previously took place. For premodernity, the extreme belief that God or the fates controlled all aspects of life, and that whatever happened to a person was from God based upon God's will and the person's response to God's will, began to lose ground with the rise of science, which saw causation in nature and science, rather than in God. Modernity could explain concepts in rational terms that had previously been unexplained or were superstitiously applied to God or religion. For example, the black plague that ravaged Europe in the Middle Ages, seen through the lens of premodernity as coming directly from God as a punishment, now had a scientific explanation within modernity; it was, in part, due to a lack of understanding of proper hygiene. Therefore, what began, in modernity, as a needed shift toward understanding science and how things work in God's world ended in a rejection of God's supernatural involvement in the world. The lens through which modernity viewed life saw all of life as one big science lab, where everything could be defined and questions answered, using science and rational thought. In many respects, God and faith were no longer seen as "rational."

The postmodern reaction to modernity was then to reject the focus upon the scientific method and rational discovery.[16] Postmodernity (1900s to present) is primarily a Western phenomenon reacting to modernity in Western civilization,[17] more specifically to the modern worldview and the effects of the Enlightenment.[18] However, postmodernity went on to claim that neither science nor an all-powerful being was the foundation for our beliefs, thus, rejecting the two foundations that supported the prior historical periods: God as the foundation for premodernity, and science and rational thought for modernity. Postmodernism claims that no foundation exists for our beliefs and life system. According to Grenz, "The postmodern ethos resists unified, all-compassing, and universally valid explanations."[19] Postmodernity as a cultural movement and postmodernism as a philosophical construct[20] no longer accepts what has previously been defined and accepted as truth, from science and rational thought to theology. In postmodernity, all metanarratives[21] are removed, and there are no claims to

---

16. Grenz, *A primer on postmodernism*, location 288 of 4319.
17. Adams, "Toward a Theological Understanding of Postmodernism," 518 – 519.
18. Grenz, *A primer on postmodernism*, location 1104 of 4319.
19. Ibid., location 288 of 4319.
20. Adams, "Toward a Theological Understanding of Postmodernism," 518–19.
21. The term "metanarrative" reflects a type of foundational "grand" narrative or

absolute truth. According to Kevin J. Vanhoozer, regarding the extremes of postmodernity, "everything becomes undecidable"[22] and nothing is knowable for certain. However, the harmful effect of a rejection of universal truth in postmodernity can also be a place to start in terms of faith and faith crises.

Postmodernity

Two characteristics of postmodernity that are important to faith crisis are the "intellectual marketplace" and the "process of deconstruction."[23] The intellectual marketplace within postmodernism reflects the newfound shared knowledge that seeks to level the playing field of authority and power structures. Knowledge is no longer thought to be held by those with power, but rather is available through such avenues as the Internet. This means, for example, that ideas that are initially taught can be challenged, because nearly everyone has instant access to the same information available to the one teaching.[24]

The second important reality of postmodernism is the process of deconstruction, which compels individuals to peel away the layers of words and ideas so "individual bits of information are extracted and separated from each other."[25] In postmodern culture, what is stated or what has always been believed is no longer acceptable as the authoritative or definitive belief. Postmodernism encourages a critical analysis of concepts down to the bare minimum and allows avenues for different interpretations of these concepts.

---

story that provides a universal claim and undergirds a society. Grenz, "A Primer on Postmodernism," Location 888 of 4319. Penner, *Christianity and the Postmodern Turn*, 127. The basics of Christian theology that God exists, God created the world, God sent God's Son Jesus who is also God to redeem humanity, serve as a metanarrative.

22. Penner, *Christianity and the Postmodern Turn*, 78.

23. Adams, "Toward a Theological Understanding of Postmodernism," 520–21.

24. Ibid., 522–23. This concept also has major implications for teachers, educators, and pastors. No longer are educators simply disseminating information only available to the one educating, as everyone has access to the same type of information. Therefore, the new pedagogical style of the postmodern generation must involve methods that allow for more critical thinking, analysis, and guided reflection and discussion rather than lecturing primarily as the means of educating.

25. Ibid., 524.

Historical Shifts in Theology

Vanhoozer explains this critical analysis as the "criticism of isms." He says, "What postmodernity bequeaths to the world is *ideology criticism: the criticism of isms*."[26] Postmodernism, by its nature, doubts and deconstructs all that "is" and no longer takes what is thought to be fact or true simply because it is said to be that way *by others*. Vanhoozer remarks:

> Postmoderns contend that claims to meaning and truth are all too often simply masks for what Nietzsche called the will to power. To say that my reading of the Bible is "true" is in fact a disguised way of saying, "This is what I *will* the Bible to mean." (author's emphasis)[27]

This means that postmodernism will be at odds with systematic theology by its very nature of rejecting claims to one "correct belief." Postmodernism lives within and is comfortable with the unknown while deconstructing, probing, and questioning life. Therefore, within our postmodern culture, more and more people are rejecting systemized theology/structure and organized religion. Postmoderns are asking questions, doubting, and deconstructing their faith. They do not merely want to be told what is true; rather, they need to experience truth personally. This personal experience, however, requires a new understanding of faith that allows for experience, relationship, and questioning. According to Jeanne Peloso, who performed a study with thirty Roman Catholic young adults on the impact of postmodernism, religion, and spirituality,

> as we reject traditional developmental notions of the self as something to be discovered, we are at a loss to explain faith development. The postmodern view of the self emphasizes the idea that the self is constructed relationally, *and there is no model of faith* which adequately addresses this dialogue. (italics added)[28]

Peloso's reference to the lack of a model of faith that addresses the postmodern culture, is what this work hopes to provide: a language and a framework for faith that seizes the opportunity our current postmodern culture provides on faith development; one that not only understands but also allows and embraces faith crises as part of spiritual growth.

---

26. Penner, *Christianity and the Postmodern Turn*, 80.; italics added.

27. Ibid.

28. Peloso, "The Theological Anthropology of Young Adult Catholics in Postmodern America," 234.

Peloso's study also reflects two important results. The first is that participants indicated that they maintained their faith in God throughout periods of suffering, though they also experienced frustration with God during those times.[29] Maintaining faith while expressing frustration with God and times of suffering helps to ground faith crisis experiences and keeps them from potentially spiraling out of control. Secondly, in expressing their faith, the group within Peloso's study indicated the need to construct a relationship with God that connected to a "revealed reality," which is another way of saying that each person needed to experience God on an individual and personal level. God must be more than an abstract thought in which a person puts blind trust. Instead, a "revealed reality" needs to connect faith with a person's experience with God.

Faith and Postmodernity

In our post-Enlightenment, postmodern world, the way society interacts with God and religion is changing. Modernity focused on mental beliefs and concepts, while postmodernity focuses on experience. Modernity emphasized the mind and the intellect over everything else, while postmodernity focuses on the entire person, including the spirit and soul. Modernity brought about systematic theology and a structured way of viewing God, while the postmodern worldview resists structure imposed by others and wants to experience God individually and communally. Modernity, largely, did not allow for questioning the status quo, while postmodernity requires it. Questions abound in postmodernity.

Postmodernity allows a degree of comfort with the unknown. Conclusions, resolutions, or facts are not required to determine systems of belief. Rather, postmodernity relies heavily upon personal experience and understanding, as do personal theology and faith crises. A faith crisis allows one to question what he or she has been told and to seek to understand for him or herself. In a faith crisis, the goal is not the resolution. Instead, a faith crisis seeks a deeper and fuller understanding of and experience with God.

Therefore, though postmodernism may contribute to the initial shaking of one's faith, due to the lack of a foundational metanarrative, it also allows for and accepts the shakiness of one's belief. Postmodernism needs no definitive belief system or support system, and it does not require that all beliefs and life systems operate off of one main concept. Without the

---

29. Ibid., 240.

pressure to believe the same thing, people are allowed to believe or not believe at their choosing, opening the door for an unprecedented time of doubt, questions, and challenges to one's faith. Where postmodernism fails in its lack of belief in a foundational belief system from which we can all find comfort and stability, it also allows for beliefs to grow, change, and deepen based upon the person's experience and understanding of God.

Postmodernism, far from the perfect philosophical construct, invites the individual to challenge, to experience, and to pursue ideas that are readily available. Deconstruction and level power-playing fields encourage people to explore and challenge basic beliefs and concepts. Though often seen as a negative result of postmodernity, this challenge to basic beliefs invites the individual to explore and experience these ideas and concepts for herself. The age of postmodernity just might provide a helpful and welcoming place for faith crises.

2

Understanding Faith

Sandy's Faith

Sandy grew up in a Christian home and was raised in church, yet found herself in the midst of a crisis later on in her marriage. After experiencing years of physical abuse from her husband, she found herself on drugs and suicidal. Though she had been a Christian all her life and genuinely loved God, she indicated that she had no encounter with who God was until the point of her desperation when she was ready to end her life.[1] As a result of her crisis, she felt hurt and angry with God, believing that God had abandoned her. According to Sandy, "When you get disappointed by God, that really leads you down a dark path. You know He's real, but He's not acting on your behalf."[2] Despite the hurt and anger, she continued to reach out to God, saying that she was in so much pain, she felt as if God understood and finally rescued her.[3] The night she planned to take her life, God intervened and she began her recovery.

In describing what faith is, Sandy said that it was being "sure of what we hope for, and certain of what we do not see." It was being "absolutely confident that God is exactly who He says He is." She went on to say that she is able to trust God in "full confidence, blindly," and that she does not "need to see it to know," that her "faith is so incredibly strong because I have seen Him over and over, prove Himself."[4] For Sandy, the mix of trusting God "blindly" along with God proving Himself were the necessary ingredients to faith. She was able at this point in her life, post-faith crisis, to trust with full confidence, not needing to know exactly how God was going to work

1. R104, digital recording.
2. R104, digital recording.
3. R104, digital recording.
4. R104, digital recording.

in her life because God had proven Himself in the past. When asked if she thought it was possible to have faith without experiencing God, she said:

> It's hard for me to, to believe that; there are people who are just totally without question, just accepting, so, it's possible. But there's something that happens that, that like turns a key, when, even though we don't see God, when we see His actions manifest in our lives, how it turns something and makes faith of a totally different level than it ever was before.[5]

Faith: What Is It?

Faith is one of those words that is complex and mysterious, yet powerful in its essence. It is ambiguous and intangible, yet full of substance, as if it were an energy source by itself. The many different descriptions and definitions of faith could and has filled many books over the past 2,000 years, but for the sake of this work, it is important to see how central a role faith plays in our relationship with God. In order to understand faith crises, we need to understand faith.

In attempting to define faith, it is often confined to an abstract concept: it is something that cannot be seen, touched, or heard, yet, somehow, we know it is there. Often, Christian theology encourages just "having faith," as if simply embracing this abstract concept without understanding it is all God requires. Additionally, faith is often defined as something one has in a certain quantity. For example, Jesus often uses the phrase, "you of *little* faith."[6] Jesus has also said, "If you have faith as *small* as a mustard seed, you can say to this mountain, 'Move from here to there' and it will move."[7] From these Scriptures, the application is that the more faith you have the better.

Faith was also an important ingredient in the life of the Old Testament patriarch Abraham. Both the author of Genesis and Paul tell us that because of Abraham's faith righteousness was credited to him.[8] Abraham had faith in a God who had probably been unknown to Abraham prior to God's call to leave his homeland and travel to a foreign land. Abraham

---

5. R104, digital recording.
6. Matt 6:30, 8:26, 14:31, 16:8, 17:20; Luke 12:28 (NIV); italics added.
7. Matt 17:20; italics added.
8. Gen 15:6; Rom 4:3.

believed in this unknown God who told him that he would bless Abraham and his progeny for generations.

In our current Christian vernacular, faith sums up our relationship with Jesus; it is how we define our salvation. John Calvin once wrote that, "Faith is not a distant view but a warm embrace of Christ."[9] For many, faith provides a warm embrace that typifies their relationship with Jesus. The familiar verse in Hebrews 11:1 that describes faith as the substance of things hoped for and the evidence of things not seen and the verse in Romans where Paul says that "the righteous will live by faith"[10] provide descriptions of a concept that is a requirement for Christians. Faith, though not completely definable or always understood, carries utmost importance for one's relationship with Christ. Therefore, when one's faith is in trouble or on shaky ground, the very core of their walk with God is seen to be in jeopardy.

Descriptions of Faith (Responses from Interviews)

Faith Described as Belief

Of the sixty people interviewed for my original study, the concept of belief or the word "belief" was used to describe faith or linked with faith in the responses of a little more than half. For the majority of those who linked belief with faith, almost a third described faith as belief in something not seen, not visible, or not tangible. For example, Paula said that faith was "belief in things that I can't quite . . . see or put my hands on, but I have a firm kind of foundation on what I believe they are."[11]

For Scott, faith is "blind trust . . . believing in pretty much anything you can't see or that's not possible, that normal people believe. Just believing what the majority don't believe in."[12] David expressed that faith is "believing whole-heartedly . . . in what you don't see,"[13] and for Samuel, it is "believing without seeing . . . in God . . . trusting that He's there, trusting

---

9. Calvin and Pringle, *Commentaries on the Epistles of Paul to the Galatians and Ephesians*, 262.
10. Rom 1:17.
11. R106, digital recording.
12. R401, digital recording.
13. R214, digital recording.

that even when things aren't good, He's still there and that He still loves me."[14] For Stacy, faith is not tangible:

> Faith is not tangible. It's believing in something . . . near yet distant. You feel and know and believe in your heart that it's near, that He is near, but yet, I feel a lot of times, too, that He's distant, but He's not . . . Faith is believing that there is more than what the world tells me.[15]

For Cindy, faith is also described as an intangible belief. Faith is a "strong and passionate belief in something that's not tangible. Something that you would, that I could easily lay down my life for but not be able to physically prove."[16] Additionally, Lisa expressed that faith is

> understanding that there is something that's out there that we can try to . . . understand for ourselves but at the end of the day, we won't understand it, but it will help us in the end. That there's a belief that you have in something that's bigger than yourself that will take care of you.[17]

These expressions of faith highlight our struggle to define the ineffable quality of faith. What these descriptions also reflect was that belief in the unseen or intangible was linked to the concept of understanding, both a lack of understanding and also coming to understand. For example, the second part of Samuel's statement about faith is, "Trusting even when I don't understand."[18] For Francis, faith is not something she can fully explain and is a "word I can't really define," but then she goes on to describe it as a belief in God.[19] Dorothy, however, indicated that a component of faith is an understanding of God's character and to "know that His intentions for us are good. Even if circumstances or what's going on doesn't look like God is working or moving, He is."[20] Though Lucille did not use the word "understand," she said that faith is a "belief of knowing."[21] Thus, some of the respondents indicated that faith is a belief in God, though not always un-

---

14. R212, digital recording.
15. R209, digital recording.
16. R121, digital recording.
17. R402, digital recording.
18. R212, digital recording.
19. R303, digital recording.
20. R308, digital recording.
21. R114, digital recording.

derstood, while others expressed faith as helpful to their understanding of God. The dichotomy is that faith helps some understand God better, while others are able to have faith even when they do not understand all that they would like to know either about God or the situation.

Faith Described as Experience

Though only a small percentage of people in the original study directly described faith with the word "experience," almost a third of the participants discussed personal experiences with God that were vital to their faith and trust in God.[22] For example, Cecilia, during a difficult time in her life, said she did not feel like God was with her, but at the same time "felt God's presence."[23] She went on to say that, "even though I felt dark and cold on the inside, I felt his presence."[24]

For Joyce, her description of "spiritual formation" reflected the need for an experience to help a person believe. She provided an example of someone who may be going through a difficult situation: "You almost need something to happen to make you like have faith or get you up again."[25] Faith in this context was equated with an event or experience that would give the person the faith he or she needed to get up and keep going.

George, several years prior to the interview, desired some kind of confirmation or audible experience with God during a time of serious health issues. He did not receive an audible response, and at the time of the interview, indicated that he struggled with whether or not God existed.[26] Whether or not an audible experience would have helped George to believe in and trust God fully, his desire for a "real" encounter with God reflects an experiential component to faith.

Lastly, Joyce said, "It's hard to explain to someone to just have faith. Trying to believe in something you can't see would be hard for someone with trust issues, but it is trusting that someone is there with you."[27] What Joyce seems to be describing is the difficulty of someone trusting in God or having faith in God without the prior experience needed to trust.

22. See Table C-1 in Appendix C.
23. R123, digital recording.
24. Ibid.
25. R108, digital recording.
26. R127, digital recording.
27. R108, digital recording.

What these interviewees each reflect is a connection between faith *in* God and experience *with* God that develops confidence in the ability to trust God. While some of the respondents described a type of "blind faith," this concept may be a contradiction; is it really possible to have blind faith if there is no prior experience upon which to trust God? The reflections from some of the interviewees seem to indicate that a component of faith needs to be connected to experiences, and that blind faith as an entire belief system is not possible for an extended period of time, if it all. Experiences in one's faith are important, and these experiences help to strengthen one's faith or to develop confidence (trust) in God.

Faith and Belief

Faith and belief are similar concepts in the Bible, and the words describing faith and belief in the New Testament come from the same Greek word, *pistis*. These two words and their connection to each other are important because it shows that, in the New Testament understanding of faith, belief and faith are interchangeable and synonymous. However, in our modern usage, faith and belief often connote different meanings. According to James Livingston, there are two different definitions of the word faith. The first definition is that faith is "a total response of a person—heart, mind, and will," or *fiducia*, which is a Latin variation for *fide* or faith.[28] The second definition for faith is reflected in the Latin word *assensus* or "intellectual assent," and in such cases is linked to belief, which in his definition is the "intellectual apprehension of a religious truth."[29] These definitions reflect the current divergent paths that the concept of faith takes: it is either an intellectual or verbal assent to a religious idea, or it is a complete embrace of this idea that owns the entire person, body, mind, and soul. While *fiducia* according to Livingston reflects an entire life centered upon faith, the second definition of *assensus* reflects a mental or intellectual grasp of the concept of faith without any action or commitment to that concept. For example, one can know intellectually that eating certain foods will cause him or her to become unhealthy over time, but knowing this concept may or may not cause that person to act upon that knowledge and be committed to a lifestyle of healthy eating.

28. Livingston, *Anatomy of the Sacred*, 289.
29. Ibid.

According to Livingston's definitions, and more accurately what seems to be our current application of the concept of faith, *fiducia* and *assensus* are ideas on the opposite ends of the faith spectrum rather than two parts of a whole. These two definitions of faith are also describing an either/or understanding of faith; it is either knowledge/mental belief, or it is an embodied way of trust and commitment. Therefore, faith and belief, though interchangeable concepts in the Bible, have become separate in our modern vernacular, largely based upon how we use and understand the word "belief."

James Fowler, in his work on *The Stages of Faith* makes a similar observation about the separation of faith and belief in our understanding of these terms today. In referencing Wilfred Cantwell Smith's description of faith, Fowler says:

> [T]he language dealing with faith in the classical writings of the major religious traditions never speaks of it in ways that can be translated by the modern meanings of belief or believing. *Rather, faith involves an alignment of the heart or will, a commitment of loyalty and trust.*[30]

According to Fowler, to say that faith is "belief" today would diminish faith to an intellectual idea or verbal acknowledgement of faith. Dallas Willard calls this a "purely mental view of faith."[31] In this context, faith's reduction to a form of cognitive affirmation of an idea or mental assent causes faith to become an idea and a verbal proclamation of the idea, merely something we mentally affirm we believe and a verbal acknowledgement of that belief. If faith is mere affirmation of an idea, then our faith rests in our ability to affirm our belief in said idea. Therefore, though belief and faith were interchangeable concepts in the Bible, they have come to mean two different things.

What further complicates our understanding of faith is the abstract and often "blind" approach with which we engage faith. As indicated earlier in this chapter, faith is a concept that we have trouble defining or understanding, and it seems as if we approach faith intuitively and even emotively, committing ourselves to faith without understanding the commitment we are making. Perhaps our modern culture has embraced this unknowable aspect of faith because faith is described in Scripture as believing in

---

30. Fowler, *Stages of Faith*, 11; italics added.
31. Willard, *The Spirit of the Disciplines*, 23.

something not seen;[32] potentially, we believe that the purest type of faith is that which is the most naïve and simple. If faith is "the substance of things hoped for and the evidence of things not seen," *our ability to believe without seeing is the measure of our faith.* "Believing without seeing" is then translated into "blind faith," which means no measure of evidence or proof is needed to trust. The more we can just accept all that we read or hear about God without understanding or without experience with this God, the greater our faith. In this way of thinking, the greatest level of faith is one that simply hears and accepts. For example, in John 20 Jesus tells Thomas that he has believed because he has been able to see Jesus' resurrected body, but blessed are those who will not able to see Jesus in the flesh and yet will still believe.[33] We might interpret this passage to mean that God requires belief in God without evidence of God's existence or experience with God. Unfortunately, in interpreting this statement by Jesus, we are missing the context of the entire chapter and the progression of faith that is illustrated.[34] As we will discover in chapter 6, the issue for Thomas was not about "proof" of Jesus' resurrection, but rather a failure to understand Jesus' mission from the start, as did the other eleven apostles.

Faith and Trust

Moreover, herein lies one of the problems with a blind or simplistic approach to faith; what we are told about God by our parents, pastor, or Sunday school teachers is based upon their understanding of God. If we grow up in a Christian household, for example, before we are even able to read we attend church and Sunday school and we are exposed to ideas about God from other people's perspective. Our understanding of God as we are growing up is based upon what others tell us even before the experience becomes our own. While hearing about God at home and at church from an early age is good, until we have an individual understanding and experience with God and our faith becomes personal, it is not formed completely and is resting upon someone else's foundation of faith. Faith for each person must become owned and formed in that person through experience, understanding, and growth, which leads to deeper trust and commitment.

32. Heb 11:1.
33. John 20:29.
34. This concept will be discussed further in chapter 6 when Thomas' story will be discussed.

Until we begin to read and study for ourselves and experience God on an individual[35] level, our understanding of God is not our own, but is based upon what others have shared with us.[36]

Faith, in a non-religious and most basic definition, is the trust and belief in something. Therefore, by itself, faith reflects the embrace of our trust, but it does not describe who or what we trust. The "who" of our trust is important, and knowing and understanding the "who" is vital to our spiritual growth. If faith is more than information that is received, and it is more than simply blindly putting our trust in something, then faith is also knowledge tied to an understanding of the object of our trust that is lived out. According to Greek definitions of faith and variations of these terms and their meanings, initial information or *epistamai*[37] (knowledge) is required to bring one to *epistemon*[38] (understanding), which can then bring one to full *pistis*[39] (faith/trust). Faith, therefore, is the ability to act on what we know about God.[40] Thus, if one's understanding of faith rests upon an idea about God[41] rather than upon confidence in what one has experienced with God, then one's faith is incomplete; it is merely one-half of the whole understanding of embodied faith.[42]

---

35. Though communal faith, i.e., the body of Christ, is also important in faith development, one of the tenants of the Christian faith is that salvation must also be individual. A person's salvation does not exist only on a communal level but must also be individual.

36. Though this concept of personal and individual faith is not a new one, I would argue that we do not understand its importance in the concept of faith. We may emphasize a person's need for her or his own personal salvation and relationship with God, but we do not understand that the salvation comes and grows through a person's individual understanding and experience with God.

37. Newman Jr., *A Concise Greek-English Dictionary*, 70.

38. Ibid.

39. Ibid., 143.

40. Personal communication with Gary Black Jr., 2013.

41. Black Jr., *The Theology of Dallas Willard*, 135.

42. A further understanding of this concept of faith involving knowledge/understanding as well as trust and lived faith can be seen in the Apostle John's writings as illustrated in *Eerdman's Bible Dictionary*. According to Eerdmans, "Once they had witnessed him perform a miracle (2:11), Jesus' disciples accepted Jesus as sent by God; others did also (v.23); cf. 4:39; 8:30), most notable upon seeing Jesus raise Lazarus from the dead (11:45; cf. 12:11). At 20:30-31 the apostle writes that he recorded many of the Master's "signs" specifically so that others might believe that Jesus was God's son. In addition to frequently linking faith with trust, John elaborates on its content. In Christian faith, people believe that Jesus is "the Christ, the Son of God" (20:31), that he came "in the flesh" (1 John 4:2), that he came from, or was sent by, God the Father (John 16:27 [cf. v.

Understanding Faith

What the interviews from this study also helped to illustrate was a connection between experience and faith that illustrates belief alone as an idea or verbal assent did not encompass fully their understanding of faith as they described experiences where God was present in their lives in some way. For a few participants, their basis of trust in God that helped to form their faith rested upon what they had seen God do in their lives or what they had experienced as it related to God. As Sandy shared in her own faith experience, "My faith is so incredibly strong because I have seen it/Him over and over where He has proven Himself."[43] Her faith, prior to her faith crisis, was built upon the foundation of others' faith. After the faith crisis, her faith was built upon her own foundation of experience and trust. The faith foundation of others is where we start and may be the catalyst for our own desire to commit to God. Yet, until we have those personal experiences and interactions with God, our only way of trusting God is based upon what others tell us God is like or has done for them.[44] Therefore, our individual faith must develop its own foundation on our experiences that invite us to trust God on a personal level.

"Right" Faith

Unfortunately, as indicated by Livingston and Fowler, Christianity has often been focused on faith as belief in an idea and thinking the "right" things. This means that when a person struggles to understand what they believe and why, the fear is that through thinking the wrong things, a person will come to believe or accept concepts that may not be correct. This focus on "right" or "correct" belief has discouraged "thinking" and analyzing our faith for fear that out of our thinking and analyzing we will begin to believe ideas about God and our faith that are not correct. Moreover, it can promote an ongoing fear about whether one has the "right" beliefs and ideas about God and thus remain on a continual search for those "right" beliefs.

When I was a teenager, I attended a Christian conference, and one of the concepts that was shared was the challenge to the Red Sea in the

---

30; 17:8]; 17:21, that he is "in" the Father (i.e., that they are one) and the Father "in" him (14:10-12), and that he is the resurrection (11:25). Such a belief includes an element of knowledge (4:42; 6:69 par. "know"), but not always empirical knowledge (20:29)." Myers, *The Eerdmans Bible Dictionary*, 374.

43. R104, digital recording.

44. Personal communication with Gary Black Jr., 2013.

Exodus story, claiming that the "Red Sea" in the Bible was really the "Sea of Reeds." According to the conference speaker, this Sea of Reeds was a small river full of reeds, in which it would have been very hard to drown Pharaoh, his army, chariots, and horsemen.[45] The speaker indicated that this challenge to biblical truth did harm to anyone who heard it, because the challenge would cause people to question whether the event ever happened and then question their faith. Putting even the thought or the question into people's minds was described as a dangerous thing, and the speaker shared his reticence even to use this illustration of the Red Sea that challenged the truth of the biblical story for fear of what it would do to the people in the audience. This challenge to the Red Sea would cause people to doubt their faith; therefore, these concepts should not be implanted in impressionable minds, or else those believing this falsehood would stray from the faith.

Although I was just a teenager, that story and caution regarding thinking about challenging concepts remained with me. The fear in my mind was not, "what if the Exodus story never happened," but rather "I should not think about things that will cause me to question or doubt my faith." The point was clear that when seeds of doubt or questions to one's faith are allowed into one's mind, the results can be detrimental to one's faith. The takeaway from that experience was never to think about things that will challenge the basis for your faith. This conference speaker was reflecting the idea that faith is largely rooted in our current understanding of belief, in ideas about God, or mental agreement to ideas about God more than it is rooted in a person's experience or trust in God. Unfortunately, the concept that was missing is that trust without experience with the object of our trust cannot really be called trust.

Scott's Story

Scott, who initially described faith as "blind trust" and "believing in anything you can't see,"[46] experienced a faith crisis when a professor at a public college challenged the existence of Jesus, claiming that no historical record of Jesus existed outside of the Bible. For Scott, this challenge sent him into a

---

45. There is ongoing debate about where the biblical Red Sea really was because the exact location of the Red Sea is unknown, and whether it was the Sea of Reeds or another body of water. In Hebrew the Red Sea is *Yam Suph*, which means "Sea of Reeds."

46. R401, digital recording.

faith spiral and caused him to doubt his faith, making him feel "horrible."[47] In order to bring himself out of this spiral, he spent time doing his own research to find out whether there were historical records of Jesus' life other than the Bible. He indicated that for him to be able to believe, finding scientific and historical evidence was important, and that the faith crisis challenging his beliefs was ultimately beneficial for his faith. He indicated that prior to the faith crisis he did not have a strong foundation for his faith. Scott's initial basis for his faith was "blind" and in something not seen, yet, when push came to shove, he needed some type of proof or evidence to ground his faith.

"Right" Understanding

It is true that knowledge itself is interconnected and built upon collaborative insight and discovery from all of humanity (there are no "new" ideas). However, in order for someone to learn rather than just absorb information, or to grow rather than simply modify one's behavior, theology must become personal and individual. Dependence upon someone else's experience or theology will not produce Christians with an embodied faith. Right belief—*orthodoxy*—alone does not automatically equate to faith; *orthodoxy* must be combined with right practice—*orthopraxy*. Yet, because the idea of belief today has morphed into a mere profession of belief, I suggest that we need to add a new term, *ortho-nous*,[48] which means "right understanding." *Orthodoxy*, *orthopraxy*, and *orthonous* must all work together to develop spiritual maturity.

Behaving in right ways and knowing what is right will not guarantee that a person has embraced his or her faith fully. Such an embrace can only come through time, experiences, and opportunities to wrestle[49] and struggle to understand God from that person's own framework. As one interviewee, Ruth, indicated she wanted to know the truth, and she could not let someone live out her faith for her.[50] If faith and belief are more than mere professions of belief in Jesus and more than a mental agreement with

---

47. R401, digital recording.

48. Greek: *ortho*=right, *nous*=understanding. Newman Jr., *A Concise Greek-English Dictionary*, 121–22.

49. More on this concept with wrestling with one's faith will be discussed in chapter 4.

50. R307, digital recording.

the life Jesus has called us to, then individuals need the time and space to come to a full or full*er* acceptance of their faith by way of their own understanding and experiences. This is why the faith crisis experience is important.

What we seem to desire today is an "experiential" faith, which speaks to one of the tenants of postmodernity and the desire for experience. Systematic theology, orthodoxy, and mental affirmations of belief have important roles to play in the church and in the faith of each Christian. However, as indicated, the problem with the focus on indoctrination as opposed to *orthonous* is that the understanding of God can stay at the level of information.[51] We do not come to an embodied faith simply from what we have been told by others. Rather, we must understand faith through our own interaction with, and study of, God. Moreover, the information that comes from right doctrine or right theology does not presume right belief, because right belief is different from simply hearing or knowing *right* information. Right belief can only take place if a person has confidence in God, which stems from experience with God, which then leads to understanding and trusting that which is true and actual about God. If information about God alone was enough to make disciples of Jesus or lovers of God, then nearly the entire world would be followers of Jesus; yet, as we know, such is not the case.

According to Dallas Willard, a lack of emphasis upon following Jesus and doing the things he did over the centuries has reduced Christianity to simply believing "proper things about Jesus."[52] A "mere mental assent to correct doctrine"[53] has defined the concept of "faith" for years, and thus we approach the concept of a faith crisis with trepidation, worrying that our ideas about an "unseen" being will be replaced with atheism as a result of our questions and doubts.

Often reduced to a mental or verbal acknowledgment of a belief, faith seems to be much more than that. While faith is not just an intellectual belief in an idea, belief is yet an important component of our faith, and belief and faith are also grounded in experience, in understanding, and in knowledge. The more we experience God, the more our trust and confidence for what God has done in the past and throughout history is likely to grow. As with all relationships and trust, our trust is built upon knowing the other

---

51. Personal communication with Gary Black Jr., 2013.
52. Willard, *The Spirit of the Disciplines*, 23.
53. Ibid.

person (not just knowing information about them), what they have done in the past, and therefore, what they are likely to do in the future.

So far, we have reflected upon a faith that forms from belief and experience out of which a personal theology is developed. Part of that experience involves an internal and cognitive shift[54] that allows one to grow in his or her understanding of God. According to Willard, "Faith grows from the experience of acting on plans and discovering God to be acting with us."[55] Faith may be initially described as a belief in an idea but must mature into trust based upon experience, which then leads to understanding. James, one of the interviewees, illustrated this by saying that the "crisis comes before the faith."[56] For him, the crisis experience was necessary for the faith to be developed. Because beliefs form our actions, what we believe about any given situation is how we will respond, unless we deliberately choose to take action contrary to what we believe. Therefore, a belief cannot be separated from our daily life or behaviors that demonstrate what we actually believe. In other words, we always act up to the level of our true beliefs.[57] Yet, faith is not just a belief, but rather a belief that we understand, experience, embrace, and live out.

---

54. Cognitive dissonance is part of the learning process in all areas of life, and will be discussed in chapter 4.

55. Willard, *The Spirit of the Disciplines*, 252.

56. R403, digital recording.

57. Black Jr., *The Theology of Dallas Willard*, 146.

3

Faith Crisis Defined

St. John of the Cross and "Dark Nights"

Before we move on to the various biblical narratives and characteristics that illustrate a faith crisis, it is important to establish what a faith crisis is. Faith crises are not new experiences, and a faith crisis is not a new concept, though it has been largely unexplored in modern theology and ministry. St. John of the Cross described a faith crisis experience several centuries ago after undergoing his own dark night and faith crisis experience.

Juan de Yepes, born into poverty, in sixteenth-century Spain, pursued a religious life, became part of the Catholic Carmelite order in Medina del Campo,[1] and changed his name to St. John of the Cross.[2] He was kidnapped, imprisoned, and tortured with the purpose of forcing him to disavow his connection to the reform movement led by Teresa of Avila.[3] It was during his imprisonment that he began to write, but his prison experience served as the impetus for his future writing titled *The Dark Night*, the work for which he is most known. A "dark night," as described by author and psychiatrist Dr. Gerald May in his book *The Dark Night of the Soul*, is marked by the realization that one is not as in control of life as one originally thinks.[4] It is a process of spiritual development, sometimes marked by tragedy, where one is unsure of what is taking place because the development is obscure or unknown—thus the meaning of the word "dark."[5] According to May, our English word "obscure" is the root meaning of the Spanish word *oscura*,

---

1. May, *The Dark Night of the Soul*, 20.
2. Mursell, *The Story of Christian Spirituality*, 208.
3. May, *The Dark Night of the Soul*, 35.
4. Ibid., 2.
5. Ibid., 4.

Faith Crisis Defined

which is translated as dark.[6] This "obscure" darkness does not necessarily imply tragedy and/or emotional darkness, such as depression, though it can in some situations, but reflects more of an inability to see clearly; things are *obscured* from vision.[7] However, because our vision of God's work in our spiritual development is obscured, the dark night of the soul can be challenging and feel "dark," but the result is a deepening of one's faith.[8]

Descriptions of Faith Crises (Responses from Interviews)

At the root, faith crises illustrate a lack of control in our faith development, as the very foundation of our faith seems to be shaking beneath us. What makes this lack of control worse is the technological age that we live in and our false sense of control over everything. Recent technological advances allow us to know what is happening, almost immediately to the time it happens. We have advanced in our ability to control our lives from health to finances; therefore, when we come face to face with reality and the parts of life that we cannot control, it can be discombobulating. Standing in the middle of a California earthquake, one quickly realizes how little he or she controls in life. While caught up in a tornado in the midwest or a hurricane on the east coast, the realization hits that there are things greater than us that we cannot control and that we do not understand completely.

Faith crises are marked by specific characteristics, one of which is doubt — doubting what one has believed about God or doubting beliefs about one's faith. Another characteristic of faith crises is questioning God or questioning aspects of one's faith. Finally, faith crises are marked by a time of cognitive dissonance,[9] or changing paradigms, regarding one's faith. Faith crises do not necessarily lead to loss of faith or belief in God, though there is an ongoing fear of such a result. The lingering question regarding faith crises is whether the faith crisis is the motivation for one to abandon his or her faith or simply used as an excuse to do so.

Interestingly, the responses from the interviews reflected that not all who exhibited faith-crisis characteristics acknowledged a faith crisis. Similarly, not all who exhibited characteristics of doubt acknowledged that they had doubted aspects of their faith. These are important distinctions,

---

6. Ibid., 26.
7. Ibid. 4-5
8. Ibid., 26.
9. This term will be discussed and defined in the next chapter.

because people may be reluctant to admit or may even be unaware of a faith crisis, despite the symptoms reflecting it as such, and they may be unwilling to acknowledge or believe that their faith is in crisis. For example, Andrew indicated that it was his child and not himself who was experiencing a crisis of faith. Yet, he described an inner turmoil where he questioned why his child was going through such a crisis because he had raised his children in a godly manner. Andrew seemed to experience a crisis of faith in which his understanding of what he believed about his faith was called into question when something was not working out the way he thought it should. Part of Andrew's theology, as he described it, reflected a belief that if he and his wife raised their kids in a certain manner and did all the things a parent should, then their children would not struggle with their faith.

Paula described her faith as "up and down" with "huge questions," such as, "Is God even real?" and "He doesn't talk to me, how do I know?" yet she did not think she had ever experienced a faith crisis.[10] Paula's original description of a crisis of faith was to "turn away from your faith, maybe not completely," and "I think it means that you are changing the way you view your faith." Paula indicated that her faith has been present most of the time. I rephrased the question to ask whether her questions or experiences had changed the way she saw her faith, and she said, "Yes, definitely." Paula could not think of a specific time when she had experienced a crisis of faith, yet, the descriptions she used, of her faith being "up and down" with "huge questions" and a change in the way she saw or experienced her faith, seem to reflect faith-crises experiences.

However, faith crises are simply points of learning and change where our understanding of an aspect of our faith is being challenged to push aside an outdated paradigm and adapt to a new way of understanding God and our relationship with God. Faith crises also illustrate such points of lack of control, or of change and changing ideas, that are often forced upon us in moments of crisis. The changing ideas, new information, and shifting events often bring us to a point of crisis because we are being challenged to adapt to this new experience, concept, or paradigm, and often the situations are beyond our control.

The results of the interviews reflected at least four common categories of faith crisis experiences:

1. Faith crises about church,

---

10. R106, digital recording.

Faith Crisis Defined

2. Faith or belief in general,
3. Theology or beliefs about some aspect of God's character, and
4. Doubt related to people.[11]

Of the sixty people interviewed, none of their faith crises involved questioning whether or not God existed. The four categories were further divided to reflect the respondents' words in describing their faith crisis. For example, though "Faith/Belief" is a broad category, some respondents simply described it by saying they questioned their faith. For example, René said that she "began to question everything she learned as a child because she had "attached her faith to her parents' truth and not necessarily the Gospel truth." As a result she had to separate what her parents believed from what she believed.[12] For René, faith was a broad category involving all aspects of her spirituality.

For some, the church or church doctrine was a significant factor in their faith crisis, as Greg's experience exemplified:

> Me: So, if I could say, your faith development
> and your, well your faith development has been,
> has been more at odds with the theology or the doctrine . . .
>
> Greg: "Exactly."
>
> Me: . . . of religion.
>
> Greg: "Exactly."
>
> Me: Than it has been with either God or the Bible.
>
> Greg: ". . . yes, exactly. It's not the Bible."[13]

Greg's faith crisis and wrestling was not with his belief in God or even belief in the Bible, but rather in church doctrine and theology.

Scott, from chapter 2, illustrated a potential doubt regarding the existence of Jesus when that existence seemed to be in question:

> Me: Tell me about that. Did . . . what did that do to your faith, your spiritual . . .

---

11. See Table C-2 in Appendix C
12. R217, digital recording.
13. R404, digital recording.

> Scott: "Made me, I don't think he made me . . . not believe, but . . . made me doubt."
>
> Me: What were some of the things . . . that challenged your faith?
>
> Scott: "I think the thing that stuck with me the most was that . . . um . . . there is, outside of the Bible there's no historical . . . historical um . . . no sign of Jesus, I guess, outside of the Bible."[14]

As you will recall, Scott's belief in the biblical account and historicity of Jesus was in question, and it caused anxiety over whether everything he believed about Jesus and the truth of the Bible was false.

For Joyce, her faith crisis was triggered by a difficult experience with her boyfriend, but out of which she gained a new understanding of God:

> Joyce: "For a few weeks I was immobile, and I didn't want to do anything." She continued, "Okay, God, what am I going to do? That was the first time I felt [God], and as if he patted me on the shoulder and said, it's okay, everything's going to be okay.
>
> Interviewer: Did it feel as if it opened a new chapter in your relationship with God?
>
> Joyce: "Yeah, it just changed my perspective on God."[15]

For Isabella, her experience was a paradigm shift in the way she viewed herself in relation to God. In describing her faith crisis, she said it was a

> critical awareness that what I have believed up to a point does not work anymore. Paradigm shift, understanding of faith in God, God's kingdom, and my role in God's kingdom changes; paradigms no longer work.[16]

The people participating in this study used vivid and similar descriptions to explain their faith crisis.[17] All of the terms used to describe their experiences represent the different perspectives and unique experiences that each person undergoes in a faith crisis. There were, however, several common themes present such as questions, challenges to God or faith, doubt, and descriptions of inner turmoil. These descriptions are important because they provide a potential template or guide for understanding

---

14. R404, digital recording.
15. R108, digital recording.
16. R116, digital recording.
17. See Table C-2 in Appendix C.

whether or not a person has, or is experiencing, a faith crisis, regardless of his or her acknowledgment of such.

The Faith Crisis Reality: Can't Avoid It

Chaos, disorder, crisis, and disarray—these words often describe faith-crises experiences. As illustrated in the table listing the various crises of faith descriptions,[18] descriptions such as "standing on Jell-O" or that it "shakes your faith" provide a visual reflection of the effect of a faith crisis. Internal faith crisis experiences are difficult to define and categorize. In such an attempt to define a person's spiritual and internal faith experience, all we have is a person's description, both their own understanding of the experience and the words they used to describe the experience, which may or may not reflect the same idea. Additionally, although some of the people indicated that they had not yet had a crisis of faith, the descriptions they used to describe their crisis experiences seemed to reflect that a faith crisis had occurred.[19] It is unfortunately possible that because we have not provided modern English language for faith crises or given people permission to experience faith crises, some people do not realize they are experiencing a faith crisis and attempt to deal with the issue in other ways. These experiences reflect inner and outer turmoil—sometimes both at the same time—as well as change, and the American Christian community needs to provide language, processes, and guideposts for dealing with these experiences.

Faith crises occur, whether acknowledged or unacknowledged, in the lives of each Christian. If faith crises are merely the process of spiritual growth or the "dark night" when we are encountering a new awareness of who God is, then every Christian experiences faith crises throughout their faith journey. *How we handle faith crises will be different for each person, but each person undergoes a process of transformation in their understanding of God and their faith in relation to God.* As we will discuss further in the next chapter, this transformation of our understanding, or what is known as cognitive dissonance, is the process of learning that allows our theology of God and our faith to grow.

---

18. See Table C-2 in Appendix C.
19. R106, 108, 112, 122, 127, 129, Digital Recordings.

4

Cognitive Dissonance and Faith Crises

As reflected in the previous chapter, there are some common indicators of a faith crisis, and a changing paradigm or "cognitive dissonance" is one of those indicators. The process of one's paradigm shift often involves an internal wrestling to adapt to the new paradigm, and there is no better way to illustrate an internal wrestling than to discuss the story of Jacob, in Genesis 32, where he physically wrestles with an unknown assailant. This story, though an actual event, also serves as a metaphor for the struggle that we experience with God during our faith journey. This story contains so much ambiguity and mystery, similar to many of the stories in Genesis: Who is this man Jacob is wrestling with, and why are they literally wrestling on the ground? Rather than giving up the fight, Jacob wrestles with this man until daybreak, refusing to let him go. As a result of this encounter, Jacob is forever changed—both physically and spiritually.

Jacob's Wrestling

Jacob's story began when he tricked his brother, Esau, out of both his birthright and his blessing. In fear for his life, he fled to Paddan Aram to stay with his uncle, Laban. Years later, as Jacob returned with his family to his homeland, he was preparing for an inevitable confrontation with Esau. This impending reunion had Jacob worried; the night before the meeting with Esau, while he was alone by the Jabbok River, Jacob met a stranger and wrestled with him.

It is revealed to Jacob that this stranger was God or God's emissary,[1] and it proved itself to be a life-changing experience for Jacob, as his body

---

1. Though the passage in Genesis continues to refer to the person as simply a man, in Genesis 32:30, Jacob realizes that it was God or an angel of God and names that place Peniel, saying, "It is because I saw God face to face, yet my life was spared" (NIV). Hosea

suffered injury that would last the rest of his life and his name was changed. In the story, Jacob refused to give up and let go, though the man told him to do so. Jacob was unwilling to let the man go until the man blessed him. He realized that there was something unique about this man, and that this man had the power to bestow a blessing upon him.

What took place next is the climax of the story: when the man asked Jacob's name. In those days, names were thought to reflect the character of a person, and Jacob was aptly named, "one who grabs a heel" or "finagler."[2] The stranger obviously knew Jacob and his name. As a result of getting Jacob to give his name, it became a type of confession of who he really was, reflecting his deceptive character and natural desire to manipulate for personal gain.[3] Though potentially attempting to overpower and "finagle" a blessing out of this supernatural being, Jacob offered a confession of his character by simply giving his name. In response to this act of honesty, the man gave Jacob a new name and, therefore, a new character as well.[4] Jacob goes from "finagler" or "deceiver" to "Israel," which means "God fights,"[5] and reflects that he "struggled with God and with men and . . . [has] overcome."[6] The word "overcome" here does not represent that Jacob has overpowered God, but rather that Jacob fought through and overcame the circumstance.

After Jacob's admission of his name, in one more potential attempt to control or overpower this man, Jacob asked the man for his name. The man replied, instead with a question, "Why do you ask my name?" thereby implying that his name was none of Jacob's business—"But nice try." In this period of history, it was believed that knowing someone's name would give you a certain amount of power over them,[7] while on an even broader scope, people of this time would use the names of their gods to manipulate their gods into doing what they wanted.[8] Therefore, it is possible that Ja-

---

12:3–4 references this story, indicating that Jacob struggled with God, then, in Hebrew parallelism, repeats this by saying Jacob struggled with the angel. Through parallelism it is reflected that the angel is synonymous with God, meaning that most likely Jacob physically wrestled with an angel, but that the angel was representing on God's behalf.

2. Hartley, *Genesis*, 236.
3. Ibid., 284.
4. Ibid.
5. Ibid.
6. Gen. 32:28
7. Armstrong, *A History of God*, 17.
8. Ibid., 22.

cob was attempting to manipulate this mysterious and ethereal being for his own benefit. The man refused to give his name, and in so doing, illustrated that God cannot be controlled or manipulated into doing what we want.

This wrestling experience, though an actual event, is also a metaphor for Jacob's internal struggle with his character, his life's choices, and God. In that encounter by the river, Jacob wrestled persistently until he received what he needed, a breakthrough and transformation. Alistair McGrath, in his work *Christian Spirituality,* indicates that within the Christian tradition the idea of struggling is an important theme:

a. A struggle with outside forces or those hostile to Christianity

b. An internal struggle against temptation

c. A struggle with God.[9]

He describes this struggle as a "desire to apprehend God fully,"[10] and links this same story of Jacob wrestling with this concept. Perhaps Jacob desired a blessing that would keep Esau from killing him or harming him and his family, or perhaps Jacob desired a curse to put on Esau if Esau tried anything. In any case, God would not be manipulated for Jacob's desires. *God did nothing to resolve the Esau problem; God only dealt with Jacob and Jacob's problems.* The real issue was not Esau and what Esau would do, but rather Jacob and the need for Jacob's character to be transformed.

Cognitive Dissonance and the Internal Struggle

Learning and then accepting a new concept can be a challenge for anyone, especially if it is related to our faith. It might be a challenge to a previously held perspective about a passage of Scripture, or it might be a new concept learned regarding other religions and how this new concept impacts belief in God or the Bible. Any new concept that is learned has to be adjusted into an old paradigm about the concept. For example, if we are told that scientists have discovered that the color of the sky is really not blue, although it appears to be, it has the potential to challenge our very understanding of colors. Everything we know about color is thrown into disarray—perhaps we even begin to feel a crisis regarding our wardrobe (Have my clothes been clashing all of my life and I have not even realized it?). If the sky is not blue,

9. McGrath, *Christian Spirituality*, 95.
10. Ibid.

Cognitive Dissonance and Faith Crises

but yellow, then is everything we think to be blue in fact yellow? Cognitive dissonance causes an internal wrestling with ideas that, in turn, cause emotional stress or anxiety. Another example is a child who previously believed in Santa Claus and learns there is no Santa Claus. If this belief was firmly entrenched in the child's mind to the point where Christmas centered on this belief, the effect of this revelation would be emotional distress, forcing the child to reevaluate what they believe.

We can all resonate with the reality of having our faith in a person challenged. Perhaps someone close to us has done something that has caused distrust, or we can remember the first time we realized our parents, teachers, and pastors were not perfect, but very fallible. Our first experiences with the imperfections of people and of the unfairness of life is what we call "the loss of innocence," similar to how Adam and Eve awoke to the harsh reality of evil after they ate of the forbidden fruit.[11] They covered up because they suddenly realized that the other human they trusted and were vulnerable with could not, in fact, be trusted completely. This awakening to the harsh realities of life is a type of faith crisis, though the objects of our faith are people and life, rather than God. The movie *Enchanted*, a recent twist on the fairytale genre in movies, portrays such a crisis. The main character experiences "wake up" calls throughout the movie as she realizes that real life is not a fairytale. In this movie, the main character comes out of a cartoon fairytale into the "real" and modern world, and has to learn how to survive. In one scene she even learns how to get angry and voices her anger at the male lead character. After her experience with the real world, she chooses to remain in the real world because the fairytale world is no longer enough to satisfy with its simplicity and innocence. What this character reflects is the loss of innocence and the cognitive dissonance that we all experience as we learn and grow.

In experiencing the disorienting effect of learning a new idea, the emotional distress or internal wrestling typically continues until a resolution of some kind takes place. Developmental scholars describe this concept as "structural development," and it occurs specifically when "the subject must construct new modes of knowing and acting in order to meet new challenges of the environment."[12] According to this idea, a new schema or model must be developed in order to have a location in which to place the new data. In order for understanding of a new concept to take place, a new

---

11. Gen 3.
12. Fowler, *Stages of faith* : 100.

construct or paradigm must be developed that allows for the new data to interact with other information.

Perspective Changes and Understanding (Responses from Interviews)

Respondents often used the word "understand" or "understanding" throughout the interviews. In nearly half of these times, it was used to discuss either an understanding of their faith or God, or a lack of understanding God/faith. One-third of the time, the term understanding was used in relation to a person's faith crisis or understanding of God in difficult times. For example, Christa indicated that her view of God changed after her faith crisis by allowing her to see "His [God's] gracious side," and that she was also able to understand God.[13] Lucille also described how her understanding of God changed after experiencing the loss of a family member. The result of this experience was, "Getting to the other side of understanding grace; I think I have a much better understanding of the freedom that we have."[14] During Yvonne's faith crisis, there were times when she felt as if even God did not understand her situation and the pain that she felt.[15]

Some other respondents did not understand why God allowed them to have such painful experiences,[16] and Lisa still questioned whether God understood the pain of her loss.[17] However, in Dorothy's case, although she initially did not understand why God was allowing a difficult situation to occur, she came to understand that God loved her.[18] Dorothy's primary understanding of what she was experiencing clouded her view of God, which seems to be part of the internal wrestling to grasp something that does not make sense. Yet, it was Dorothy's understanding of God's love that helped to resolve her crisis. She did not have a resolution to the "why" question, which people tend to seek, but she did have an understanding of God's love. Understanding the primary importance of God's love was illustrated

---

13. R119, digital recording.
14. R113, digital recording.
15. R101, digital recording.
16. R126, R308, digital recording.
17. R207, digital recording.
18. R308, digital recording.

by Philip, who, while describing faith, said that it was more important to believe that God is love even than to believe that God exists.[19]

Greg came to realize that before his faith crisis, he was a "zealot"—pointing fingers and judging others. After his faith crisis, his perspective of his theology of God changed.[20] He was also initially discouraged by others in his attempt to understand God and ask questions. When he tried to ask his pastors questions that he had about God or his faith, they responded by telling him that he cannot understand God, which tends to reflect a common response in evangelical Christianity.

Lastly, some of those interviewed reflected that there were aspects of God and their faith that they either did not understand or could not understand, but that a lack of understanding was part of the faith process.[21] These people had come to accept that understanding all aspects of their faith was not always possible.

A faith crisis is related to one's belief system, which in turn is related to one's paradigm of how he or she views faith and/or God. The cognitive dissonance that takes place within the faith crisis reflects the struggle to understand and adapt new experiences and concepts to old paradigms, and understanding is often the end of the cognitive dissonance experience.

Crisis and Cognitive Development

In a study of crisis in pedagogy[22] and religion, Philip Tite discusses how crisis involving religious studies and a person's faith is necessary for learning in an academic environment. Tite believes that, when students encounter a challenge to previously held beliefs and assumptions, they are experiencing a "crisis of cognitive dissonance."[23] The crisis is an internal challenge to previously held assumptions and beliefs. He goes on to say, "Dissonance emerges, I would contend, due to a type of paradigm shift."[24] Tite states, "Rather than defusing crisis, I argue that we should nurture and encourage

---

19. R210, digital recording.
20. R404, digital recording.
21. R108, R201, R208, R212, R124.
22. Pedagogy refers to the various styles and methods of teaching, and it involves the study and application of teaching.
23. Tite, "On the Necessity of Crisis," 79.
24. Ibid.

students to engage those moments, for through such engagement comes learning."[25]

For Tite, this "dissonance" is necessary for a paradigm shift to take place within the student. This process of cognitive dissonance causes students to become open to a new way of understanding and knowing, from one "cognitive space to another cognitive space."[26] He argues that the crisis a student may experience is both unavoidable and beneficial. However, the cognitive movement taking place in this experience is only a change in direction or mode of cognition, not a change from a primitive to superior way of thinking.[27] The student is not moving to a "smarter" or more advanced way of thinking, but perhaps a deeper way of thinking, or even a willingness to accept the dissonance that comes from different ways of "knowing" religion and his or her belief system. According to Tite:

> What we are faced with is differing, and seemingly conflicting, ways of knowing (faith knowing, i.e., confessional or prescriptive, and non-faith knowing), in conjunction with the movement from one way of knowing to another way of knowing.[28]

This illustrates the hoped-for result in cognitive dissonance: rather than creating a vacuum of *not knowing*, coming to understand concepts in different ways enlarges one's paradigm to allow for new information to integrate with old. What Tite explains is the need to accept the internal crisis and thus allow for a new way of understanding concepts and beliefs. Faith crises are a type of cognitive dissonance within a person's belief system, challenging a person to shift the way one thinks about one's faith.[29]

---

25. Ibid., 76.
26. Ibid., 80.
27. Ibid., 82.
28. Ibid., 80.

29. Cognitive growth and new ways of knowing are key components in spiritual formation. If in a faith crisis a person's way of understanding his or her faith is being questioned, cognitive dissonance will occur and the person will be challenged to explore new ways of viewing faith. However, in order for one's faith to be challenged in a way that promotes growth, an understanding of faith itself is important. Yet, as discussed in chapter 2, in the evangelical tradition there seems to be an emphasis upon faith that is mere intellectual assent, *assensus*. This *assensus* faith in Christian and evangelical theology seems to be based upon the Scripture in Hebrews 11:1, "Faith is being sure of what we hope for and certain of what we do not see," as is reflected in my data as being the most common Scripture used to define one's faith. However, faith is also seen by some as not blind trust or just intellectual assent but, rather, as dependent upon an initial experience or encounter from which belief evolves and leads to faith. This view of faith illustrates

Faith Development Theory

Tite's proposed necessity of cognitive crisis in the classroom, and the movement from one type of knowing to another, is directly connected to Faith Development Theory (FDT). FDT has its roots in James Fowler's work, *Stages of Faith*. As a psychologist and practical theologian, Fowler opened the door for a new study on the concept of developmental faith.[30] According to Fowler, "faith is a verb; it is an active mode of being and committing, a way of moving into and giving shape to our experiences of life."[31] For Fowler, faith is active, not static, and faith operates in stages of movement or, in some instances, regression. Additionally, as is true in other developmental models, a person may or may not journey to, or through, each of the faith stages. In FDT, people do not simply move to the next stage at a certain period in their life, and some do not move past a certain stage once they have reached it. This is important because one of the questions my original research sought to answer is whether faith crises are important in a person's spiritual formation, which can be synonymous to faith development. An important concept for further study is whether faith crises are part of how our faith grows and whether these crises are necessary for a person's spiritual development.

Fowler's faith model consists of six stages:

a. Intuitive Projective Faith

b. Mythic-Literal Faith

c. Synthetic-Conventional Faith

d. Individuative-Reflective Faith

e. Conjunctive Faith

f. Universalizing Faith.[32]

---

that faith operates to some extent on a visible or tangible level, that it is not purely an unseen or unknowable spiritual reality in our lives. According to Black Jr.'s description of Dallas Willard's theology, "Rather, belief is only the first step that must proceed toward the development and eventual establishment of an interactive knowledge of the reality of God and his character." *The Theology of Dallas Willard*, 145.

30. Fowler relies upon Erik Erickson's and Jean Piaget's development models in his Faith Development Theory, as well as Lawrence Kohlberg and H. Richard Niebuhr. Although others have built upon this model of spiritual growth, Fowler is the first who was well known in the modern age to introduce a detailed model and to tie this model effectively to other sciences, such as developmental theories. Fowler, *Stages of faith*, 159–60.

31. Ibid., 16.

32. Ibid., 16. It is important to note that Fowler argues very few people ever reach

Although all of the stages are important in understanding how faith develops, for the purpose of this project, only stages 4 and 5, Individuative-Reflective Faith and Conjunctive Faith, will be discussed briefly.

Individuative-Reflective Faith (Young Adulthood and beyond)

In the fourth stage, Fowler described the internal processes as a type of "cognitive narcissism":

> Frequently overconfident in their conscious awareness, persons of this stage attend minimally to unconscious factors that influence their judgments and behavior. This excessive confidence in the conscious mind and in critical thought reflective self over—assimilates "reality and the perspectives of others into its worldview.[33]

In this stage, the individual reaches a point of full, or as near full as possible, awareness about his or her self and others and begins to examine his or her own beliefs. A person may find himself challenging what he has believed through the years, his concept surrounding God, and whether he completely agrees with what he has always believed. Reflection, introspection, evaluation, and analysis of who a person is, who God is, and how these concepts relate to each other are important in this stage. *This stage reflects a time of questioning*, when all a person believes may be questioned, which can be challenging and disconcerting. Additionally, the descriptors of this fourth stage seem to be the same as in a faith crisis. If this is true, it is possible that faith crises are necessary in order to progress to the next stage of faith development.

Conjunctive Faith (Early Midlife and beyond)

In this second-to-last stage, a person learns to adjust to the tensions and conflicts in life and faith, rather than seeing reality as either/or, or black/white, as in the first stage. In Conjunctive Faith, a person learns to accept the multiple facets and angles from which situations and life overall should

---

the final stage, or have reached this stage. To illustrate the type of people who *might* be in this stage, Fowler lists examples like Mahatma Gandhi, Mother Theresa, Thomas Merton, and Martin Luther King Jr. Ibid., 201–3.

33. Fowler, *Faithful Change*, 63.

be viewed.³⁴ While in the previous stage (Individuative-Reflective Faith), a person demythologizes faith while seeking to determine what is true or real, in this fifth Conjunctive Faith stage, a person moves beyond the demythologizing and comes to accept ritual, symbols, and other aspects of the religious experience.³⁵

In the Conjunctive Faith stage, a person may not necessarily reinstate old beliefs, yet does not feel the need to continue to *deconstruct* said beliefs, which is characteristic of the previous stage (as well as the postmodern movement in general). Instead, a person in this fifth stage may choose to accept some previously held beliefs and determine how those beliefs fit into her new understanding of faith, religion, and God. The Individuative-Reflective stage involves deconstructing belief, while the Conjunctive Faith stage involves constructing, and at times reconstructing, beliefs within a new framework.

The concept of reconstructing beliefs was detailed by Paul Ricoeur in his discussion of the first naiveté, critical distance, and then second naiveté.³⁶ Ricoeur described a process whereby a person learns first in uncritical acceptance of ideas (first naiveté), then begins to evaluate critically the concepts learned (critical distance), and then progresses to a second naiveté in which "critique and full reception coexist and enhance one another."³⁷ Our understanding of ideas grows from initially accepting what we hear (simply believing everything we read or are told) to analyzing whether we believe these ideas or whether they are in fact true.

Fowler connected Ricoeur's second or "willed" naiveté to his Conjunctive stage, indicating that "persons of the Conjunctive stage manifest a readiness to enter into the rich dwellings of meaning that true symbols, ritual, and myth offer."³⁸ A person's willed naiveté indicates that she is no longer ignorant of what she believes, but rather she is choosing to see faith as something that does not necessarily have to be proven for all to examine and see. This willed naiveté reflects a type of acceptance and/or resolution to the internal conflict through accepting what she did not know before.

These fourth and fifth stages of faith development illustrate a period of growth from potential crisis to acceptance: questioning and wrestling

---

34. Ibid., 65.
35. Ibid.
36. Ricœur, *The Symbolism of Evil*, 351–52.
37. Frohlich, "Spiritual Discipline, Discipline of Spirituality," 78.
38. Fowler, *Faithful Change*, 65.

(Individuative-Reflective), which can then lead to a period of acceptance (Conjunctive Faith) where beliefs have not necessarily been proven or defined; rather, the person accepts both what is known and what may not yet be known. The resolution is not the proof of any religious existence, experience, or solution to any crisis experience, but the belief or faith in the wholeness of God.

Therefore, the internal crisis one experiences from a faith crisis is the cognitive dissonance of trying to understand the new concept and its place in one's paradigm. As reflected by Tite earlier, the dissonance comes about due to a person's shifting paradigm.[39] According to Gay Holcomb and Arthur Nonneman, anything that causes one to question what he or she believes and why, and causes an active engagement with his or her roles or ideologies is a crisis.[40] This is where Ricoeur's concept of "critical distance" comes into focus whereby a person figuratively removes himself/herself from the idea that is in flux and evaluates how that idea can or will fit into his/her schema.[41]

The Cognitive Dissonance Cycle of the Psalms

The disorientation that takes effect in the faith crisis seems to find a commonality in the book of Psalms. In his work on the Psalms, Walter Brueggemann finds a pattern that relates to a faith crisis that indicates a normative pattern for faith development and spiritual formation overall, with disorientation as the middle stage of crisis.[42] Brueggemann's cycle of orientation, disorientation, and new orientation is visible throughout the psalms and reflects:

a. Equilibrium (orientation),

b. Disequilibrium as a result of change, crises, difficulties (disorientation), and then

c. Homeostasis once again or equilibrium (new orientation).[43]

---

39. Tite, "On the Necessity of Crisis," 79.
40. Holcomb and Nonneman, "Faithful Change," 100.
41. Ricœur, *The Symbolism of Evil*, 351–52.
42. Brueggemann, *The Message of the Psalms*, 21.
43. Ibid.

Cognitive Dissonance and Faith Crises

Brueggemann insightfully illustrates a pattern that is not just typical in faith crises but is typical of life overall.[44] As discussed previously, developmental growth of all kinds requires a kind of change[45] that often brings disequilibrium or disorientation from the normal status and a movement toward a resolution of the change that brings about equilibrium once again.

Yet, the cycle, as it comes back to a kind of equilibrium, is not built upon the previous structure that caused equilibrium or orientation, which is why Brueggemann calls this final stop in the cycle "new orientation." Once a person has processed or experienced the disorientation, her experience causes growth beyond her previous understanding that held homeostasis; equilibrium is now held with the new understanding based upon experiences and new knowledge. According to Brueggemann, "That new orientation is not a return to the old stable orientation, for there is no such going back. The psalms know that we can never go home again."[46] There may not be an "old stable orientation," but there is a new stable orientation that has been shaped by experience and understanding, as some of the participants illustrated in their new understanding of God and how it shaped their faith as a result of the crisis.

This cycle of orientation, disorientation, and new orientation is illustrative of the kind of movement that takes place in a faith crisis.[47] Though this study did not examine, in detail, the after-effects of a faith crisis or whether there was a resolution to the crisis, it was clear that a new understanding or new way of viewing God was *a* or *the* primary result of the faith crisis. The resolution of the crisis of faith was not necessarily an answer to all of the person's questions or prayers, but it was a new way of understanding God.

Cognitive Dissonance and Changing Views of God

The result of a faith crisis is a change in one's view of God and understanding of his/her relationship with God. Therefore, a person wrestles with the new experience or new concept to try and fit it into his or her cognitive schema. Whether the change is drastic or slight, the faith crisis disrupts

---

44. Ibid.
45. Fowler, *Stages of Faith*, 100.
46. Brueggemann, *The Message of the Psalms*, 124.
47. Ricoeur's first naiveté, critical distance, and second naiveté can also be compared to this cycle.

previous paradigms or schemas, causing them to shift to make way for a new perspective of God. The changing paradigm is often disconcerting, uncomfortable, and outright disorienting, yet, unless our understanding of God changes, we will be stuck in old paradigms of God that may reflect an incomplete view of God.

C. S. Lewis, in his *A Grief Observed*, makes this observation about the changing view of God, "Images of the Holy easily become holy images-sacrosanct. My idea of God is not a divine idea. It has to be shattered time after time. He shatters it Himself." He goes on to say, "Could we not almost say that this shattering is one of the marks of God's presence? The incarnation is the supreme example; it leaves all previous ideas of the Messiah in ruins."[48] Lewis acknowledges the shattering or shaking of one's faith that seems to be required for any kind of growth. The concept of who God is must be shattered or, at the least, shaken so that it can be reformed to provide a better glimpse of who God actually is. The process of reforming that paradigm of God is difficult and can be lengthy, yet it is the process of growth as God redesigns and informs a deeper understanding of who God is.

As illustrated by Fowler's discussion of the faith stages, changing views of God take place as a result of growth through the various stages of faith. The example of Santa Claus illustrated earlier applies in this context because a child will view God from a more magical and mystical framework, similar to her view of Santa Claus. As a child is growing, the perspective of God changes to encompass more attributes of God than just a benevolent or jolly friend. Yet, the obvious result of a lack of deeper understanding and knowledge of God in a person's faith is debilitating, and here is where the comparison between Santa Claus and God ends. As children grow into adulthood, most who are healthy will abandon the belief in the idea of a Santa Claus because he does not exist. However, a child's faith in God must grow and deepen as he or she matures; otherwise, the child will come to a point where God may be cast off just as quickly as other mystical figures. As we mature and grow in developmental stages, so will our faith or understanding of God, if we allow it. If we do not allow our faith or understanding of God to deepen and grow, we may reject any notion of God, or at the very least, we will not come to understand the depth of God's nature.

Faith crisis involves a change in our understanding of God, yet because God is perfect and God does not fail us, our faith crisis regarding God stems from *our* lack of understanding of who God is, not God's imperfections

---

48. Lewis, *The Complete C.S. Lewis Signature Classics*, 684.

or failures. Our faith crisis in people revolves around the revelation that people are not perfect and will fail us. Yet, with God, our faith crisis cannot stem from God's imperfections because God is perfect; rather it stems from our misunderstanding, or a small paradigm that does not fully grasp who God is. As we will see in the next chapter, theodicy can sometimes come from a realization of suffering and trying to understand how our previously held beliefs about a good God are reconciled with pain and suffering.

When our faith crisis involves experiences with church, though we are not necessarily challenging our belief about God, it can be equally challenging. The church is often the lens through which we see and interpret God, and we tend to see the church as God's institution and way of connecting with us. Therefore, for many, the church is a reflection of God and their relationship with God. Several of the people I interviewed had issues with the church, and it was their struggle with the church that affected their faith crisis and their relationship with God. For at least two of the people I interviewed, their present struggle with God was a result of the hurt and experiences they had within the local church.

A faith crisis, though it can imply a tragic experience where one is in danger of losing his or her faith, is not always the case and may be a sign of a changing view of God. Therefore, faith crises are more common than we realize. For some, this change takes place in dramatic fashion and is highly charged and emotional. For others, it is more subtle and ongoing, and the inner turmoil is slight. Regardless of how a person experiences a faith crisis, it represents a change/shift in the way God is seen; therefore, it is both normative and essential for growth in faith development.

"Let Me Get There"

A TV show I was watching recently portrayed one of the main characters coming to a mental breakthrough in understanding a concept. Another character was about to help this person out by completing the thought for them, but the main character said, "Let me get there," as if to say, "Don't help me out; I want to verbalize this understanding on my own." The phrase "Let me get there" became the catch phrase for that particular episode and repeated similar experiences of each individual desiring to state or come to the conclusion on their own. These characters were exhibiting the need that we all have to arrive at breakthroughs or points of learning on our own rather than be told what the conclusion or realization of the issue is.

Too often we are not allowed to arrive at the realization or "eureka" moment on our own because other well-meaning and well-intentioned people want to tell us what the conclusion or point of learning should be. After all, why watch someone struggle to understand a concept or an issue when we already know the answer? The butterfly struggling to come out of the cocoon seems to need our help, and those of us watching the poor butterfly may be tempted to help it out by trying to open the cocoon to assist the butterfly through its struggle. Yet, as we know, it is through the struggle and wrestling within the cocoon that the butterfly's wings are strengthened, and when it fully emerges, it is able to fly unhindered in its beautiful new body. The butterfly needs to struggle within the cocoon in order to fly after it is out. The same is true for all of us when it comes to learning new concepts; we need to struggle and wrestle to understand new and challenging concepts, whether they are a change in the way we see God, or they are a change in the way we see ourselves and the world.

Cognitive dissonance, which illustrates part of the faith crisis process, although a disorienting, frustrating, challenging, and potentially even painful process, is important for our spiritual development because it is the way in which we learn and grow. If we can grasp that part of our spiritual development involves times of disorientation in order for our understanding of God to grow, it can provide a sense of normalcy in times that are abnormal or disconcerting.

5
Questioning God and Theodicy

Isabella's Theodicy

Isabella is married, highly educated, and is successful in her profession. She grew up in church and has been a strong Christian for most of her life. Her faith crisis began when a close family member, though educated and qualified, struggled to find employment following the Great Recession of 2008. Despite the fact that this person loved God and had, seemingly, done all the right things, and despite how hard Isabella prayed, her family member struggled to provide for their family. Witnessing this difficulty with her family member caused Isabella to become angry at God; she even stopped praying for a while. As with many who found themselves struggling to survive economically after 2008, the fault was not their own. Therefore, why was it that others were prospering and finding employment when Isabella's family member could not?

What is important to note is that Isabella felt comfortable enough in her relationship with God to be upset at God, believing that God was failing her family in such a needed way. When prayers of this nature go unanswered or are answered with a definitive "no," anger or frustration is a natural response. Isabella was not asking for trivial things; she was simply praying for a job for her family member who desperately needed work. How could God not respond and provide a job? For many Christians, the unanswered prayers or "no" responses for things that are needed can often provide the most angst, frustration, anger, and even depression. We may be able, at times, to interpret unanswered prayers or responses to our prayers that are different from what we prayed for, as God ultimately working for good on our behalf, or God knowing that what we are praying for is not what is best for us, despite our felt need for it. Yet, knowing these things does not necessarily resolve the frustration, fear, or anger that may ensue as we struggle to understand why we are going through what we are.[1]

Questions within Faith (Responses from Interviews)

A significant theme that emerged from the research of the sixty people interviewed was the concept of questions that arise in difficult experiences. Almost half of those interviewed, indicated that they questioned God or their faith in some way.[2] Cindy was born into a Catholic family and raised in church. As an adult, she did not attend church until her mother passed away; that became the impetus to once again connect with God and her faith. Before committing to church, however, she brought her questions about her Catholic beliefs to a priest. When asked if her faith would be as solid as it is today if she had not questioned earlier, Cindy said, "No. Many Catholics' faith is not deep because they don't question."[3]

Sandy, from chapter 2, described a crisis of faith as a time when you "question your faith, challenge, go to a place where you had to realize, do I believe or do I not?" She went on to say, "I have been there [in a faith crisis moment] and experienced that crisis of faith. God met me there. Sometimes we let things get to a point of crisis, but I am glad that I got there because it changed my life."[4]

Yvonne went through a serious and debilitating depression that seemed to come out of nowhere and was not something she could control or make go away. She and her husband had served in ministry and were faithful to God and serving in the church, so when her depression hit, it felt as if God had abandoned her. She shared three different questions that she wrestled with during her crisis: "Why am I being punished," "If I can't function as a human being, why is God keeping me here," and "Why can't God just teach me in an easier way?" She illustrates the multitude of questions that a person may wrestle with in difficult circumstances, regardless of whether these questions are verbalized or merely internalized.

---

1. After the interview, in a follow-up discussion, Isabella indicated that she began to talk to God again, though it took several months, and eventually her family member found full-time work after two years.
2. See Table C-3 in Appendix C.
3. R121, digital recording.
4. R104, digital recording.

Questioning God and Theodicy

Finally, Paula, who described her faith as experiencing "ups and downs" and contained "huge questions,"[5] indicated that she needs to either experience faith or see it experienced in other people for her to believe. Her faith needed a connection with experience, and the questions seem to precede the experience because, in her words, she does not "take things at face value."[6] There was also a direct correlation between questioning and doubting:[7] "Doubt, to me, means questioning. I think it's my way of working through the situation or the issue that's come up." She goes on to indicate that doubt is positive, "because if you don't question anything, then you are just being blind."[8]

The act of questioning, whether questioning God or the circumstances, is part and parcel to our response in the midst of a faith crisis; in fact, questioning life is part of our existence. From childhood, we pester our parents and other adults with questions (for some of us even more so) about why and how things happen, as our cognitive development grows, and we attempt to make sense of the world. Questions are simply part of our maturation process. Although the kinds of questions change as we mature, the importance of questions remains. In a world where a missing flight, such as Malaysia flight 370 can disappear and cause so much commotion, it is clear that we expect answers to life's questions and mysteries. The commotion from this missing plane is not just because of the overwhelming loss of three hundred people, it is because we have a hard time believing today that objects, like a plane, can seemingly vanish. Losing a plane may have been a bit more commonplace fifty or sixty years ago, but today, when nearly all of our movements can be tracked, we find it hard to believe that we cannot find a hundred-ton plane. In the weeks following its disappearance, news outlets ran non-stop coverage of this missing airliner. Although most ignored and shrugged off the more conspiracy-like theories, the reality of what happened was stranger still: How is it possible to lose an airliner in 2014? How do those families struggle to cope with life and so many unanswered questions?[9]

---

5. R106, digital recording.

6. R106, digital recording.

7. Doubting as an important component of the faith-crisis experience will be discussed more thoroughly in chapter 6.

8. R106, digital recording.

9. "Malaysia flight 370 took off from the country of Malaysia on March 9, 2014, and, as of the time of this writing, has yet to be found.

Unanswered questions and lack of resolutions plague all of us because we all desire closure. Few of us like to read books, watch television shows, or see movies with no closure or defined conclusion. One or two unresolved plots in fictitious works may be okay to give the plot creativity; yet, on the whole, we demand closure, especially in the many subplots of our own lives. However, the longer we live, the more we realize that life rarely wraps itself up in a neat conclusion. The more we interact with life and its tragedies, the unresolved or the unknown, the more questions we might have. In fact, it seems as if life leaves us with more questions than it does answers. However, the uncertainty of life that brings our questions to the forefront and our need to understand is a place where our faith can start. For those with faith in the reality of an all-powerful, all-knowing, and all-present God, as Christian theology defines, our faith in this being can sometimes clash with these unresolved questions. Yet, these questions do not have to be a place where our faith ends or ceases to exist, but can be an invitation into a new and deeper faith, one that accepts the mysteries and challenges of life while also seeking to understand, a faith where the questions, the doubts, and the challenges to faith are received and welcomed.

Theodicy

Theodicy is a term used to describe experiences when one attempts to understand the ways of God, particularly in moments of tragedy and suffering.[10] It is a theological term used to "justify the goodness and omnipotence of God in the face of the world's real evil."[11] Theodicy has various applications but is typically applied to suffering or traumatic experiences, when one struggles to understand God in the midst of that suffering. It asks the question, "How can we understand God in the midst of pain and suffering, especially when it seems unjust or unwarranted?"

James Livingston proposed four categories to define Christian views of theodicy: (a) Suffering as Recompense for Sin,[12] (b) Suffering as a Test/Necessary for Soul-Growth,[13] (c) Theodicy of Submission,[14] and (d)

---

10. Livingston, *Anatomy of the Sacred*, 235.
11. Ibid.
12. Ibid., 247.
13. Ibid., 248.
14. Ibid., 250.

Questioning God and Theodicy

Theodicy of Protest.[15] Christians connect suffering to one or more of these views, whether or not they are aware of the term theodicy. In order to process the suffering a person experiences, the Christian will often attempt to understand why, and how God fits in to this "why" question. Theodicy, in its simplest terms, is a "catch-all" for times of questioning in one's faith or questioning God as a result of suffering.

Job's Theodicy

Theodicy is not a new concept and is even evident in the Bible. The entire book of Job, for example, provides a great illustration of not only a crisis of faith but of theodicy. Job, the righteous man, experienced suffering because Satan wanted to tempt him into denouncing God in the midst of crisis. He lost almost everything, including his health, and suffers for a significant length of time until God restores to Job what was taken and even more. However, the way Job was written indicates that the story and experience were designed precisely to address the concept of suffering and justice in an unjust world.

The first two chapters of the book of Job describe the narrative of his tragic situation, then Job begins to voice his frustration and anger over his situation. Chapters 3–37 record a combination of Job's discourses, containing questions and directing anger toward God and anyone else who would listen, and the responses of his "friends" who were not very supportive during Job's crisis. Job voices the obvious questions of why and "what have I done to deserve this." Job goes from being wealthy, with a big family, and in good health, to having nothing. Only his wife was left, and his body wasting away from diseases. Therefore, Job does not hold back as he rails against both God and the world over the tragedy that had befallen him.

For the majority of the book, God allows Job and, unfortunately, Job's friends, the space to unburden and express the frustration, emotions, and doubt to challenge God and God's character. Finally, in Job 38:1, it says that God answered Job "out of the storm,"[16] illustrating both the literal and metaphorical storm that represented Job's present situation. Yet, God does not respond to any of the issues that Job brings up, and God never responds to Job's questions directly. According to Randall O'Brien, it is as if Job's suffering and the justice of God are irrelevant to this narrative because they are

15. Ibid., 252.
16. NIV.

not addressed.[17] However, God indirectly communicates to Job that God's ways are beyond Job and too powerful for Job to even comprehend. The result, according to O'Brien, is that "the speeches of Yahweh mysteriously result in the apparent transformation of an angry Job to one who is at peace with God."[18]

Though God never explains the reasoning for Job's suffering (this has only been revealed to the reader) and God never directly answers any of Job's questions, Job responds to God's address by saying, "My ears had heard of you but now my eyes have seen you. Therefore I despise myself and repent in dust and ashes."[19] It is a curious exchange, which is followed by God returning to Job twofold what had been taken from him, and then punishing Job's friends for neglecting to comfort him. Job does not receive the answers to his questions, but as a result of this theophany,[20] he finds peace.

Questioning God?

When I was a child, a guest speaker at my church told us about his tragic experience: the loss of his wife as well as other family members in a car accident. As he relayed the story and the difficulty of coping with the loss, he said that even through all of this tragedy, he "never asked God why." Although he had experienced such a tragedy, he clearly felt that asking God why would challenge God's sovereignty and would have, therefore, been a bad thing.

The concept of asking God "why" in tragic situations as a bad thing to do, has always remained with me, and it brings up important theological questions: Do we as humans have the right to question God's judgement or why he allows the things in life that he does? Is it impudence to think that God should respond to us and give us a reason for why God does the things God does or why God allows the things God does? Who are we to question God?

---

17. O'Brien, "World, Winds, and Whirlwinds," 152.
18. Ibid.
19. Job 42:5–6, NIV.
20. The word "theophany" is used to describe a direct encounter with God in one of the physical senses: auditory, visual, etc., or with an angel representing God. It relates a manifestation of God to humans.

Questioning God and Theodicy

God's response to Job has always brought up questions and different interpretations as to what God is saying to Job and whether God is chastising Job for his questions. We may look at God's response and see a heartless one, one that never seems to sympathize with Job, or even an implied concept that questioning God is wrong. Job challenged God throughout most of the book and God responds with:

> Who is this that darkens counsel by words without knowledge?
>
> Brace yourself like a man; I will question you, and you shall answer me.[21]
>
> Would you discredit my justice?
>
> Would you condemn me to justify yourself?[22]

Such statements by God seem to imply Job's audacity at even hinting that God was wrong to allow what was happening to Job. God is also turning the tables on Job, as it was Job who was initially challenging and questioning God, but God responds by saying, "Now you will answer *me*." God meets Job's challenge with a revelation of who God is rather than addressing the specifics of Job's many questions. According to O'Brien, Job challenges God's goodness, morality, and justice while acknowledging God's wisdom and power. Yet, God, in God's response to Job, only discusses God's wisdom and God's power while ignoring Job's challenge to God's goodness, morality, and justice.[23]

There are no apologies from God about the trials inflicted on Job, but there is a revelation of who God is. God is an unknowable, all-powerful, and completely separate entity. Had God defended God's self and justified why God allowed these things to happen, it could have reduced God to a being who simply exists to serve our wants, similar to a magic genie that we control with our wishes. O'Brien indicates that from this narrative we see that "God owes no one of us any more than God has given us. All is gift. Life is gift. Life is grace."[24] God withholds the details of events, not because God cannot or does not want to provide them, as though God is withholding vital information and only dispenses such information on God's whims, but rather because we cannot understand. God declared God's sovereignty and God's "God-ness," which are concepts that are well-beyond our ability

---

21. Job 38:2–3, NIV.
22. 40:8.
23. O'Brien, "World, winds, and whirlwinds," 154.
24. Ibid., 156.

to comprehend. The end of the book illustrates whether Job can accept what he cannot understand, whether he will trust God despite the trials and challenges. It also unveils a perspective change and transformation on Job's part.[25]

What is important to remember is that Job was the only one who was unpunished at the end of this story.[26] If Job's questioning of God was wrong, it seems unlikely that God would have responded with the blessings that were heaped upon Job.[27] Additionally, the purpose of this test was to see if Job would turn his back on God, which he did not, but rather, he directed his complaint *to* God. God's goodness and fairness were being challenged, and God responds. Job walks away with an understanding that God is God, wholly other and separate from humanity and life, yet, a God who cares enough to respond.

Being reminded of who God is, is often what we need when the storms of life hit. In similar situations, we may never know exactly why something happened; more often than not, we do not receive the answer to our why. The why, it seems, cannot be answered, either because we as humans cannot understand it or because there is no answer.

The Brunt of Our Frustration

It may feel sacrilegious to demand answers of God, but if our faith is based less on a belief in a higher being and more on a relationship of trust with this being, then moments of doubt and question in that relationship are part of forming that trust. When Isabella could not make something happen by either working at it herself or praying for it to happen, her natural response was to pull away from God. After all, what good are such promises as "ask and you will receive"[28] if we do not receive the thing for which we are asking?

The difference between a faith crisis about life or other humans and a faith crisis regarding God is that God is perfect and cannot act imperfectly.

---

25. Ibid., 157.

26. Job 42:7–10.

27. Job 42:10–17. The Bible also contains other instances of people challenging God: for example, Abraham, who bargained with God over Sodom and Gomorrah (Gen 18:16–33), and Moses, who challenged God's desire to wipe out the children of Israel because they would not obey God (Exod 32:11–14).

28. Luke 11:9.

Questioning God and Theodicy

Our Christian theology based upon our biblical theology says that God does not make mistakes and that God cannot "fail us" or "let us down." However, when God allows bad things to happen to us or does not answer our prayers the way we want God to, it is perceived as "letting us down." The angst and frustration stem from the tension that what we are experiencing is what we prayed against or we did not receive what we prayed for, clashing against the concept that God does not fail people, make mistakes, or act imperfectly. It may also be clashing against the many promises from the Bible that God will bless, provide, and give to God's people. Job's faith crisis could have stemmed from a belief that if he followed God in a righteous manner, God would bless him. This belief seems to be rooted in the Old Testament law, particularly in Deuteronomy: "If you follow me, I will bless you. . . . " Job was wrestling with what appeared to him as a failure on God's part to protect him and keep him safe. It can be incredibly frustrating when we realize that most things, including God, are not in our control.[29] Not being able to express frustration to the person with whom we are frustrated is counter to the concept of building trust within this relationship with God.

God is often the target of our anger and hurt for our own issues. I consistently encounter people who cannot reconcile the concept of a loving God in a very painful and broken world. Some of them direct their anger and frustration at God for God's lack of compassion and action in this broken world; who else can we blame for things that are out of our control—death, natural disasters, diseases, plagues—than someone or something who is all-powerful and all-knowing? When there is no human to be blamed, we desire to take our anger and hurt to someone who has the power to stop what no one else can.

Theodicy, Pain, and Paradigm Shifts

In struggling to reconcile our understanding of God in the midst of pain and tragedy, we can reduce God and God's actions to something we can comprehend. Questions such as, "Why would God punish the entire human race for something that two people did in the Garden of Eden thousands of years ago," and "Why doesn't God intervene in tragic situations such as the

---

29. The concept of "control" in our relationship with God brings up many additional questions: To what extent does control and our inability to control God play into our times of doubt and questioning? How many faith-crisis moments are due to unanswered prayer and our inability to control the outcome of a situation?

Holocaust" are attempts to reconcile what we have been taught about God: that God is just and loving. In response to these issues, theologians will refer to original sin and the freedom with which humanity has the power to interact with society. Others who have attempted to tackle this question come back to the concept of God's sovereignty and omniscience, that God knows more than we will ever know and that this is something we cannot possibly understand. There is truth in understanding God's sovereignty and omniscience while trying to grapple with the issues of suffering. According to Randall O'Brien, in order to understand human suffering and theodicy, our ethical basis must be reoriented and reframed from anthropocentric to theocentric.[30] In reference to James Gustafson's *Ethics from a Theocentric Perspective*, O'Brien is saying that biblical morality is centered upon God's will, not humanity's will. Rather than viewing morality as what is right and good for humanity only, it views God and God's care and concern for God's entire creation, past, present, and future, as the ultimate value.[31] What a theocentric worldview reflects is the basic concept we see in God's response to Job, that God is wholly other, separate, and beyond our understanding; there is an element of "Father knows best" in God's actions.

For example, it is common to be self-focused in our prayers, relying upon Scriptures that tell us to ask and pray for the things that we need.[32] There is a constant struggle with our selfish desires and what is best for our lives,[33] and we are not always aware of how our prayers will ultimately affect us or even others. Hezekiah, in the Old Testament, is a great example of how prayer affects others. Hezekiah was a king in the southern kingdom of Judah. When God told him through the prophet Isaiah that he would die soon, Hezekiah cried out to God, with less of an "asking for mercy" prayer focus and more of a "Why me?" and "What have I done to deserve this?" focus.[34] God allows an extension of his life, but it is in this extended time in Hezekiah's life that Manasseh, Hezekiah's evil son, was born.

Prayer reflects a reality of God intervening in a situation, which involves Isaac Newton's third law of motion. This law says that for every action, there is an equal and opposite reaction. If I pray to get a specific job, I am praying that I get this job over any other person who also wants the job;

---

30. O'Brien, "World, Winds, and Whirlwinds," 156.
31. Ibid., 158.
32. Matt 7:7–8; Luke 11:9–10.
33. Jas 4.
34. 2 Kgs 20.

Questioning God and Theodicy

if I get the job, someone else will not. This does not imply that our prayers are consciously myopic nor does this imply that there are not enough jobs to go around. However, practically speaking, five people are applying for the same job and my prayer is to get that job, I am praying that I will get the job and someone else will not. When God acts on our behalf, God is going against some law of nature or free will, which makes it miraculous. Free will and how it interacts with society is complex, with the interlocking, web-like matrices that connect all of life. C. S. Lewis discusses this concept in his *The Problem of Pain* by saying:

> That God can and does, on occasions, modify the behaviour of matter and produce what we call miracles, is part of Christian faith; but the very concept of a common, and therefore stable, world, demands that these occasions should be extremely rare.[35]

The dichotomy is that, as Christians, we believe in miracles and God's ability and desire to interact with the world; yet miracles also affect free will and the orderly world God has set in place. God granted Hezekiah's prayer, yet, it allowed time for his son to be born, and who largely receives the blame for the Jewish people going into captivity.[36] The very miracle I am hoping God will grant me might not be the thing I really need and it might actually be harmful for me and others. Prayer, a wonderful and important component of our relationship with God, has the potential to alter the affairs of the world and may also involve God directly contravening someone's intentions or actions.

In *A Grief Observed*, Lewis wrestled with his own understanding of theodicy. His book was written as a result of his own loss and suffering after his wife passed away:

> The more we believe that God hurts only to heal, the less we can believe that there is any use in begging for tenderness. A cruel man might be bribed—might grow tired of his vile sport—might have a temporary fit of mercy, as alcoholics have fits of sobriety. But suppose that what you are up against is a surgeon whose intentions are wholly good. The kinder and more conscientious he is, the more inexorably he will go on cutting. If he yielded to your entreaties, if he stopped before the operation was complete, all the pain up to that point would have been useless."[37]

---

35. Lewis, *The Complete C.S. Lewis Signature Classics*, 565.
36. 2 Kgs 23:26.
37. Lewis, *The Complete C.S. Lewis Signature Classics*, 674.

Lewis is making the case for the necessity of pain in our lives and that God, as the perfect healer, has to inflict or allow pain because it is part of a larger picture of our own healing that we do not always fully understand. Lewis seems to be arguing that suffering is a test or a means for soul growth.[38] The case Lewis makes is both theologically and intellectually sound and it helped him find meaning in his grief. Though making an intellectual and theological argument, Lewis is also writing from experience. Before he could come to this resignation of understanding God and pain, he first wrestled with such questions as "Where is God?" and "Why is He so present a commander in our time of prosperity and so very absent a help in time of trouble?"[39] He noted that Jesus himself exclaimed "My God, my God, why have you forsaken me?"[40]

Lewis goes on to say:

> Not that I am (I think) in much danger of ceasing to believe in God. The real danger is of coming to believe such dreadful things about Him. The conclusion I dread is not "So there's no God after all," but "So this is what God's really like. Deceive yourself no longer."[41]

He is expressing an honesty that some may struggle to verbalize or even acknowledge, yet they still may feel deep down. Similar to Job, Lewis seems to be willing to lay his questions and pain open before God, willingly acknowledging that he is doubting God's love in that time and place. By the end of his book, Lewis has come to understand God and pain a little more and has at the very least, come to a place where he can find some comfort in believing that God is using pain for his good.

Similar to both Lewis and Job, those in the middle of a tragedy, struggling to find peace and make sense of suffering, must experience God for themselves *before* they can rest in the idea that God is good. It is one thing to know intellectually this aspect of God's goodness,[42] but it is quite another thing to be in the midst of pain and tragedy and not be able to feel the goodness of God. God's goodness is not just an intellectual pursuit; it requires

---

38. Livingston, *Anatomy of the Sacred*, 248.
39. Lewis, *The Complete C.S. Lewis Signature Classics*, 658.
40. Ibid. Matt 27:46; NIV.
41. Ibid.
42. Though some do not see God's goodness in all of God's actions, God's goodness is not dependent upon our perception because God is still good despite our perception or our circumstances.

orthonous, right understanding of God that goes beyond intellectual or verbal agreement, and that is rooted in the experience of God. It is arguable that one cannot know of God's goodness until one experiences God's goodness in the midst of pain and suffering, which does not feel like God's goodness at the time. Moreover, God's goodness may never, in fact, "feel good." Yet, through our increasing experiences with God, we come to understand both who God is and the larger reality in which God operates, and we find ourselves resting in the ultimate reality of God. This ultimate reality goes beyond our own experiences, which may never reveal themselves to be positive (those who experience abject horror in life and die as a result are never able to experience the "positive" or good from that experience in this life), but again, we rest in the understanding of who God is and how our lives fit in this broken world that God desires to redeem.

The phrase by Lewis, "any use in begging for tenderness" illustrates the harsh truth of growth, which is that growth involves pain. The book of James in the New Testament discusses this concept by saying, "Consider it pure joy . . . when you face trials of many kinds." And Hebrews speaks of a similar concept, "No discipline seems pleasant at the time, but painful. Later on, however, it produces a harvest of righteousness and pace for those who have been trained by it."[43] In moments of honesty, we might acknowledge that our difficult and painful experiences in life have caused growth and we can trust that these Scriptures are true—that God will perform necessary growth surgeries in our pain and tragedy, and so we hold on to these things.

Regardless of whether suffering is brought about by God for our good or allowed by God for our good, we must be able to struggle with the suffering in a way that helps us understand the situation and, most importantly, experientially understand that God is, in fact, working for our good, despite tragedy. It is one thing to know God intellectually; it is another to know God experientially.

---

43. Jas 1:1; Heb 12:11 (NIV).

6

Doubt and Faith Crises

KNOWING GOD EXPERIENTIALLY OFTEN involves times of questions and times of doubt. Doubt plays an important role in faith crisis right along with questions or questioning aspects of one's faith. Interestingly, in my study, more people seemed to acknowledge some form of questioning God or their faith than they had acknowledged times of doubt (though whether or not someone had doubted was one of the questions used in the interview). It is possible that those who fear either questioning God or doubting God worry that they will become atheists. Yet, as reflected in the previous chapter, for those like C. S. Lewis after he lost his wife, he indicated that his worry was not in ceasing to believe that God existed, but that he would come to believe awful things about God and God's character.[1] However, fear from expressing doubt toward God may come from an understanding of certain Scriptures that seem to define faith as "never having doubts" about God or one's faith. The Gospels record Jesus teaching on the smallest amount of faith needed, such as a mustard seed, telling Thomas to "stop doubting and believe,"[2] and chastising his disciples numerous times for having "little faith."[3]

The accepted interpretation of these Scriptures seems to be that faith must always be strong, and even when we feel our faith is shaking or struggling, we must *pretend* to have faith because that is what God seems to require. Rather than believe God wants our genuine emotions and thoughts, we feel the need to pretend even with God that our faith is not experiencing any times of doubt, struggle, or questioning. If Jesus chastises his disciples for their "little faith," then we must always exhibit strong or much faith. We may come to believe that God wants us to act always as if we had faith,

1. Lewis, *The Complete C.S. Lewis Signature Classics*, 658.
2. John 20:27 (NIV).
3. Matt 6:30, 8:26, 14:31, 16:8, 17:20; Luke 12:28.

because somehow the adage "Fake it till you make it" also applies to faith. If we act as if we have faith, then faith will somehow come.[4] We may have no faith whatsoever, but if we "fake" that we have it, God will honor our attempt and bless us or meet our need.

Christian Reflections on Doubt

Faith, according to Neal Krause, by its very nature, particularly in the Christian faith, requires a belief in the unseen.[5] The Christian faith is based upon supernatural events involving a God who cannot be seen, though is believed to be present in human form in history and is held to have died and then risen from the dead. Therefore, questions such as the following become important as we study faith crises and their effects: To what extent is doubt involved in a person's faith crisis? And is doubt embraced, rejected, or denied in the faith crisis?

In order to address these questions, it is important to understand how doubt has been viewed in Christian theology. In the Christian community, both academic and non-academic, religious doubt has been viewed from two opposite perspectives: either doubt is not helpful and should be avoided (this seems to be the consensus amongst most Christians), or doubt is a good and necessary aspect of faith development and growth.[6] In an attempt to destigmatize the concept of doubt and allow for its acceptance into theology, Ronald Habermas wrote an article titled, "Doubt is not a Four-Letter Word."[7] He used the definition of doubt given by Paul De Vries, namely, "the act of questioning, the expression of uncertainty. Doubt is the humility of the mind asking real questions and seeking real solutions."[8] Habermas also used Philip Phenix's categories of doubt, which describe

---

4. I am not referencing the concept that sometimes we need to act despite how we feel because our feelings do not determine reality. There are definitely times when our faith is "little" or shaky, yet we need to move forward despite our doubt and fear. What I am discussing here is the denial of our emotions and concerns rather than the honest acknowledgment of our doubt and fears.

5. Krause, "Religious Doubt and Psychological Well-being," 94.

6. Ibid., 95.

7. Habermas, "Doubt Is Not a Four-Letter Word."

8. Ibid., 402.

both "constructive" and "destructive" doubt, illustrating that doubt alone is not destructive, but rather is shaped by how a person engages in doubt.[9]

Opposing Habermas's definition of faith, two researchers, Neal Krause and Keith Wulff, tested the relationship between religious doubt and health. The purpose of their study was to show the negative effects of doubt on one's faith, and in a nationwide sample of respondents, the research revealed that doubting one's faith was directly related to high depression rates and negative effects on a person's health.[10] The study also confirmed Krause and Wulff's hypothesis that those who occupy formal roles in the church have more significant problems in the areas of depression and physical health.[11]

However, there were two specific limitations of their study, which were acknowledged by the researchers: the fact that the data have no longitudinal perspective, and that the surveys were only administered to people who were attending church during the last week in April 2001.[12] Krause and Wulff acknowledge that those who may have left the church *because of doubt* and/or those not present during the time the research was performed would not have participated in the study.

There is an additional limitation of Krause and Wulff's study: it does not take into account each person's definition of doubt. This is important because if one's understanding of doubt or questioning of faith is held to be wrong or "sinful," he or she may be prone to feel distress or a sense of guilt over the doubt. This is particularly true for those in a position of leadership in the church. According to Krause and Wulff:

> Instead, individuals who are more involved in the church (i.e., people who hold formal roles in the church) appear to have the most difficulty with religious doubt. This makes sense because people with the deepest levels of commitment to religion, and those who are more involved in it, have the most to lose if their religious beliefs are called in question.[13]

Krause and Wulff also acknowledged that the *types of doubt* were not measured; for example, one may doubt a doctrine at a specific church but not the broader implications of his or her religious faith.[14] What was mea-

9. Ibid., 403.
10. Krause and Wulff, "Religious Doubt and Health," 50–51.
11. Ibid., 48.
12. Ibid., 52–53
13. Ibid., 51.
14. Ibid.

sured was the existence of doubt and whether or not it affected one's health or well-being in a negative way. *Moreover, if doubt is seen as a negative part of one's faith, the attempt to avoid or suppress doubt may be part of the cause of the negative effects on one's health.* In a following study involving doubt and psychological well-being, Krause admitted that a person's reflection on his or her well-being may not be an accurate measure for whether or not the doubt was helpful.[15]

In a follow-up study, Krause engaged in a survey of adults that examined the connection between doubt and a person's well-being, specifically, a person's psychological well-being.[16] He found negative correlations between doubt and psychological well-being, specifically that religious doubt causes a diminished sense of well-being over time, and that older adults with more education are more likely to experience religious doubt.[17] Krause did find, however, that although adults with more education are more likely to doubt, they are less likely to suffer from the adverse effects that adults with less education might experience.[18] These adverse effects include the belief that doubt is wrong and, therefore, should be denied or repressed, which creates less willingness to forgive oneself if doubts arise.[19] The fact that the adults who were more educated experienced more times of doubting, yet experienced less of the negative effects of doubting than the uneducated adults, reflects a correlation between education and the doubting experience. It seems possible that those persons who have a higher level of critical thinking, whether educated or not, may be more willing to engage in doubt. It is also important to consider whether denial and suppression of doubt potentially keep one from growing spiritually in difficult experiences.

In the same way that Krause and Wulff's study has illustrated an adverse connection between doubt and a person's health, Krause showed a negative correlation between doubt and one's psychological well-being. Yet, Krause's study identified *psychological stressors* as the negative aspect of doubt, which means that a person's perspective on his or her well-being *is the measurement for the negative* or "deleterious effects"[20] of religious doubt

---

15. Krause, "Religious Doubt and Psychological Well-being," 106.
16. Ibid., 95.
17. Ibid., 105.
18. Ibid.
19. Ibid. 105-106
20. Ibid., 106.

on a person's faith, rather than a scientific or quantifiable measurement of negative effects.

The accuracy of a person's self report on his or her own well-being is called into question, particularly if it is the determining qualifier as to whether there is a positive or negative result from the doubt. A person's psychological expression is subjective, based upon a person's evaluation of his or her emotions at a given point. A person's temperament or personality, his or her faith commitment, and other variables that may influence a person's response, were not factored into Krause's study.

Moreover, as indicated by Krause and Wulff's study on doubt and health, if doubt is perceived by the individual to be a negative concept from the start, a person experiencing it will likely experience distress. The doubt causes the distress based upon a person's understanding of it. Therefore, it is important to note that both spiritual growth and a person's psychological well-being are vague standards of measurement as they are mainly subjective in nature. Krause went on to say, "Perhaps the point of wrestling with doubt is not to be content, satisfied, or happy—*instead it may simply be to learn.*"[21]

Krause and Wulff's combined study, as well as Krause's study on psychological well-being, both reflected the negative effects of doubt and religion. However, a study conducted by Puffer and others at Indiana Wesleyan University on 604 adolescents from the midwest found positive correlations between adolescents' ability to doubt and the development of their ideology or identity.[22] More specifically, they found, "doubt is associated with a motivating identity consciousness compelling persons to explore."[23] Over the years of study on adolescent development, it has become understood that adolescence is the age of discovery and exploration as youth are questioning and examining their beliefs on every level, particularly those of an existential nature.[24] The authors conclude:

> If a genuine and vibrant identity cannot emerge without exploration and doubt is linked to this criteria, then doubt of any kind (religious, political, etc.) appears to be related to healthy psychological development.[25]

21. Ibid.; italics added.
22. Puffer et al., "Religious Doubt and Identity Formation," 278.
23. Ibid.
24. Ibid., 273.
25. Ibid., 278.

Doubt and Faith Crises

The insights from Puffer and his collaborators on adolescent doubt have brought to light the varying views of religious doubt: those who think doubt either dangerous at the most or annoying at the very least, and those who believe doubt to be important for "faith maturation."[26]

An additional component to the study of religious doubt takes place within the current postmodern culture and its willingness to question and deconstruct everything. According to Puffer et al.:

> Jones (2001) profiled Christian post-moderns as persons who deconstruct the known by questioning everything, assuming nothing, and taking nothing for granted, habits which often lead them to be skeptical and cynical.[27]

Postmodernity[28] and its effect on Christianity is an important component of faith crisis, since a postmodern worldview naturally lends itself toward a more fluid and questioning system of belief. This connection to a postmodern society brings up the question of whether doubt can ever be avoided if questioning has become a vital characteristic of a postmodern society. If, according to Puffer and his collaborators, doubt correlates with a desire to explore, then that exploration can potentially lead to new understanding of one's faith, and thus, spiritual growth.

From these studies we can see that how we perceive doubt, whether good or bad, will determine the extent to which we acknowledge that we have doubted or allow ourselves to doubt. Moreover, if church theology reflects a negative understanding of doubt, doubt experiences will be discouraged and potentially not acknowledged by the person who is experiencing doubt.

Reflections on Doubt from Interviews

Regarding those who doubt and may not want to acknowledge it or those who experience fear when doubting, three respondents discussed either a personal fear or avoidance of doubt, with one of the three indicating that Christians simply are afraid to doubt. Julie, in particular, stated that she did not doubt, but then went on to say that she was afraid to doubt because she

---

26. Ibid., 270.
27. Ibid. 270-271
28. Postmodernity is discussed in detail in chapter 1.

did not want to let God down.[29] René mentioned that she thought Christians have a fear that if they doubt, they will become atheists.[30] Though doubt involves questioning and people seem more ready to question than doubt, the negative responses to doubt may reflect the fear that doubt is or leads to disbelief, and that, if a person doubts, he or she will lose or has lost his or her faith. Natasha reflected on the fact that she was not "allowed" to question her faith because her parents feared that she would lose her faith.[31]

Aaron described a crisis of faith as similar to "standing on Jell-O,"[32] and seven other respondents used the term "shaky" to describe the foundation of faith in a crisis of faith. These descriptions illustrate the understandable fear of experiencing a crisis of faith if one's foundation does not seem as secure or firm. Fifteen of the respondents who were asked to define a crisis of faith described it using words such as "doubt" or "questioning."

Twenty-one participants expressed that they had experienced some type of doubt in their crisis experience. For example, Tommy indicated that "There are moments in my life that I have doubt, and moments that I have, you know, not a lack of faith, 'cuz I definitely have a lot of faith to push it to the side."[33] Don reflected the importance of doubt by saying, "Anybody who's never doubted deeply I don't think has ever believed deeply."[34] Similarly, Dorothy, doubted her "view of God," but did not doubt whether God loved her.[35]

However, for some, doubt seemed to reflect a negative aspect of faith, and these participants were less inclined to express that they had doubted their faith. Seven of the respondents described the phrase in negative terms, using such descriptions as "losing one's faith," or "turning away from God." Eight indicated that they did not doubt their faith, and some responded by saying they doubted others or themselves more than they doubted God.[36] Lynn shared that doubt played a big role in her recent illness, but proceeded

---

29. R105, digital recording.
30. R217, digital recording.
31. R122, digital recording.
32. R125, digital recording.
33. R205, digital recording.
34. R305, digital recording.
35. R308, digital recording.
36. See Table C-3 in Appendix C.

to describe doubt in the doctors, nurses, and even friendships, rather than a doubt in God or her faith.[37]

Natasha illustrated the negative reflection of doubt by saying that, to her, doubt meant that "you have no faith or hope."[38] Additionally, Christa said that she doubted God's promise to her was enough, yet she was "scared to voice those times of doubt" and did not "want to give voice to the doubt."[39] Thus, Christa expressed the ambivalence that seems connected to doubting.

Doubt vs. Unbelief

So far, we have seen that faith-crisis experiences involve questioning and doubting and, often as a result, guilt. Yet, because doubt is too often seen in a negative light, uncovering crisis moments fully in our present society may not be completely possible; those who experience such questioning moments may not want to admit it to others or possibly even to themselves. Ronald Habermas made this statement regarding doubt and questioning:

> Most Christians claim that queries about faith are negative, writing off all forms of doubt as the antithesis of belief. Nothing could be further from the truth. As a result, however, the church has suffered greatly from this well-accepted misbelief.[40]

According to Habermas, not embracing or seeking to understand all aspects of our faith, including the questioning times and doubting moments, can do significant harm in our attempts to face openly uncomfortable and disorienting experiences.

Habermas goes on to quote Paul de Vries of Wheaton College on the role of doubt in one's faith. According to Habermas, de Vries says, "Doubt is the act of questioning, the expression of uncertainty. Doubt is the humility of the mind asking real questions and seeking real solutions. Surely one can believe and question at the same time."[41] De Vries goes on to make a comparison between doubt and unbelief: "In its biblical usage, 'unbelief' always connotes stubborn resistance, disobedience, and rebellion. In short,

---

37. R115, digital recording.
38. R122, digital recording.
39. R119, digital recording.
40. Habermas, "Doubt is Not a Four-Letter Word," 402.
41. Ibid.

doubt is the sincere question, but *un*belief is the *un*willingness to hear the answer."[42]

This kind of "stubborn resistance" can be seen in Mark 6 with Jesus' hometown that rejected him simply because they knew him. Despite hearing his wisdom and seeing or hearing about his miracles,[43] the people from his hometown rejected him and took "offense" at him.[44] Jesus' response to their unwillingness to understand or believe was that he was "amazed at their unbelief." The New International Version translates the word "unbelief" as "lack of faith," but the New King James, the New American Standard, and the New Revised Standard versions all keep the word "unbelief," thus making a distinction from the passages that we discussed earlier regarding "little faith" and "unbelief." These three versions are connecting with the context of this passage in Mark 6 and the motives of the people. Their struggle with belief in Mark 6 was not due to a desire to believe and having difficulty in doing so; rather, it was a refusal to believe what was right in front of them, what they saw and heard for themselves.

Another story from the New Testament helps us to see the differentiation between unbelief and doubt. The story of Thomas in John 20, although seeming to reflect Thomas's refusal to believe what was right in front of him, was actually a different kind of struggle to believe and reflects a longer narrative of the process that one's faith can take as it matures.

Reclaiming Doubt and the Story of Thomas

The story of "doubting Thomas" in John 20 is a familiar story often used to denounce faith crises, or, more specifically, doubting. Reflected in the unfortunate moniker received because of such doubting, Thomas is the disciple who initially refused to believe that his master had risen, until he could see him with his own eyes. His story is often used as a cautionary tale against the act of doubting as it relates to faith.

42. Ibid.; author's italics.

43. What is both amazing and hypocritical is that the people saw his miracles and heard his teaching, yet, *still* rejected him. According to Mark 6:2–3, "On the sabbath he began to teach in the synagogue, and many who heard him were astounded. They said, "Where did this man get all this? What is this wisdom that has been given to him? What deeds of power are being done by his hands! 3 Is not this the carpenter, the son of Mary and brother of James and Joses and Judas and Simon, and are not his sisters here with us?" And they took offense at him" (NRSV).

44. Mark 6:3 (NRSV).

However, what if we were to look at this story in a different way? Rather than imposing two thousand years of assumptions regarding doubt and Thomas upon this story, what if we were to look at his struggle as a faith crisis rather than a stubborn or rebellious refusal to believe? Thomas was the only apostle that we know of who refused to accept the word of others that Jesus was alive. He does not appear to be ostracized by the others; yet, he is the only one to challenge the testimony of those who said they saw Christ resurrected. It is important to note that he is not challenging his own experience with Jesus post-resurrection; he is challenging what *others have told him*. As indicated earlier, it seems we are taught that we are to have faith regardless of our feelings, experiences, or concerns, and if one does not believe and have faith at the moment, he or she should at least pretend to believe. Therefore, the teaching of this story implies that Thomas should have simply pretended that he had faith and "chosen" to believe the others' story about Jesus being alive, rather than voice his concern. After all, what was wrong with Thomas that he could not believe what was so obviously true?

What seems to have been forgotten in this larger story of the apostles during Jesus' ministry and after his death is that none of the apostles initially understood that Jesus was going to be resurrected, which is why they were hiding out in a locked room, worried that they were next. John 20:9, referencing specifically Peter and John but also indirectly referencing all of the apostles, says, "for as yet they did not understand the scripture, that he must rise from the dead."[45] For example, when Peter attempts to stop Jesus' arrest by cutting off the apprehending soldier's ear, he did so because he did not understand what was happening. Jesus had to be arrested so that he could be put on trial, so that he could die for our sins, so that he could resurrect from the dead, and so that he could prove himself the divine Messiah. Yet, Peter and the other apostles were viewing Jesus from an outdated and false paradigm of an earthly messiah who would overthrow the Roman government and set up an earthly kingdom.

Additionally, we forget in the story of Thomas in John 20 that the other apostles had the opportunity to see Jesus alive before Thomas did. Jesus came and appeared to all the apostles except Judas Iscariot, who had committed suicide by this time, and Thomas, who for some reason was absent at this first appearance. Why Thomas was not there the first time, we simply do not know. Maybe he was in a state of despair, struggling even

---

45. NRSV.

to be around others. For whatever reason, Thomas was not present during Jesus' first visit. Moreover, for some, like Peter and John, this was the second time they had the opportunity to see Jesus. Putting ourselves in the place of Thomas, we can empathize with his frustration when everyone else seems to be having miraculous experiences, hearing God's voice so clearly, or experiencing God's presence in intimate ways; yet, we struggle to hear and see what seems to be so obvious to others. By the time Thomas comes to the room again, he is hearing these experiences that people have had with Jesus, and he is the only one left out—the only one who has not experienced Jesus *for himself*.

Personal experiences are exactly what seem to be taking place in John 20. What I have discovered in this chapter is not only the emphasis upon the various aspects of coming to faith but also the story's illustration of the role of experience in each person's life as he or she comes to believe. John places Thomas's experience in the context of three other people's encounter with the risen Christ and illustrates a progression of belief, starting with John himself and ending with all who have yet to come and will not see Jesus in this life, but will believe.

Progression of Belief in John 20

Person	Action
Peter	Entering the tomb (vv. 6–7)
John	Seeing then entering the tomb (vv. 5, 8)
Mary	Hearing Jesus call her by name (v. 16)
Thomas	Seeing Jesus for himself (vv. 26–28)
The Reader	Reading and believing the narrative (v. 29)

The story reveals Peter and John rushing to the tomb after Mary Magdalene told them that the tomb was empty. Both disciples needed to see the tomb up close, but Peter's passion propels him impetuously into the tomb,

Doubt and Faith Crises

he looks around, and he seems to believe. John reaches the tomb before Peter, but cautiously pauses and sees everything first, including the empty linen wrappings, but it is not until he goes inside that he believes.[46]

Mary stayed at the tomb while Peter and John went back to share the good news with the other disciples. While waiting at the tomb, Jesus appears to Mary and has a conversation with her, though she was unaware that it was Jesus speaking with her. John writes that it is not until Jesus simply calls her by name, "Mary," that she recognizes him and cries out, "Rabbi!" Finally, Thomas, who refused to believe that Jesus had risen until he could touch him personally, sees the risen Christ and believes.[47] Kelli O'Brian, in discussing these passages states:

> Believing in the Fourth Gospel goes beyond intellectual content to something more fundamental: acceptance of Jesus and willingness to remain with him despite difficulties of all kinds, including uncertainty about precisely what it is that Jesus is revealing.[48]

When viewed from the entire Gospel of John, Thomas is painted as more than simply a fearful doubter. According to J. H. Charlesworth, "Thomas is not a doubter; he is the reliable realist . . . He is no duped enthusiast; he is the self-reflective and thoughtful, even courageous, leader."[49] Thomas is mentioned in two other passages in John's Gospel. In the first passage, Thomas challenges the other disciples to go with Jesus so that they could "die with him."[50] The second passage describes Thomas's questioning Jesus regarding how to get where he is going.[51] Jesus declares that he is going away and preparing a place for them, but Thomas wants to make sure that they know where he is going so that they can follow him. He asks, "Lord, we don't know where you are going, so how can we know the way?" Jesus responds with one of the great pillars of the Christian faith that he is "the way, the truth, and the life."[52] Stan Harstine makes a similar case for Thomas:

---

46. John 20:8
47. John 20:26–28.
48. O'Brien, "Written That You May Believe," 291.
49. Harstine, "Un-doubting Thomas," 445–46.
50. John 11:16.
51. John 14:5–6.
52. Ibid.

> Would Thomas's resistance to swear loyalty *to anyone proclaiming to be Jesus raised from the dead* have been viewed as unbelief regarding Jesus' identity? Would the loyal character who desires to follow Jesus but does not know where to go (John 14:1–7) so quickly replace his loyalty with doubt? When given proof of his identity would the disciple willing to follow Jesus to Bethany so that he might die with him (John 11:16), suddenly refuse to accept this one? Would this disciple characterized previously as loyal and faithful easily exchange his fidelity for doubt and mistrust?[53]

Does Thomas exhibit the doubt of disbelief or the doubt of someone who wants to know and wants to believe? As mentioned earlier, none of the disciples understood what Jesus came to do and thus they ran away when he was arrested and were in mourning when he died. Thomas, the realist, wanted to be sure; he questioned, he wanted something more, he needed something more to resolve the inner turmoil he was experiencing. He was being told Jesus was alive, yet he did not understand why that would be true because his understanding of Jesus as the Messiah coming to free the Jewish people from Roman oppression was a paradigm that was faulty and, quite simply, too small. Thomas was experiencing a crisis of faith, and the resolution would not come until he gained knowledge and experience of the risen Jesus for himself.

One of the powerful concepts that emerges from the story of Thomas is his new understanding of who Jesus was. Thomas uttered "My Lord and my God" when this knowledge was achieved. This is the first utterance of a declaration of Jesus' divinity by someone other than Jesus.[54] From this unique experience with Jesus, Thomas was able to move past a mere "Jewish Messiah" concept of Jesus. He does not refer to Jesus as the Christ or Messiah, but instead recognizes that Jesus was, in fact, God, and Jesus' mission was much broader than the Jewish people previously understood. Thomas makes a declaration that illustrates he finally understands who Jesus is. Jesus was not the deliverer that his disciples hoped he would be, rescuing them from Roman rule; Jesus was God, coming to establish God's kingdom on earth, redeeming humanity, and showing the way to the gospel or the good news of the kingdom. Thomas's new understanding came after the struggle, the wrestling, and the doubt. It may have taken Thomas a while

---

53. Harstine, "Un-doubting Thomas," 447; italics added.

54. I was first introduced to this concept on the novelty of Thomas's proclamation from a lecture by Elizabeth Talbot on the "Gospels Witness to Christ" course at Azusa Pacific University, School of Theology, 2007.

to understand Jesus, yet when he understood, his knowledge was catalytic and transformative.

Although Jesus tells Thomas to "not doubt but believe," the progression of belief and coming to faith in the chapter implies that Jesus is encouraging Thomas to put away the doubt he has been struggling with and finally believe. Thomas has experienced Jesus for himself and uttered the recognition of Jesus that no one else had expressed at this point in the gospel narrative;[55] now Thomas can let go of his doubt and believe.

---

55. Ibid.

7

Losing Faith: The Fear and Danger

HAVING GROWN UP IN church and served in pastoral leadership for many years, I have experienced the ongoing concern over watching people struggle with their faith, fearing that they will abandon their faith and walk away from God. As discussed previously, there is a difference between doubt and unbelief, and lack of faith and unbelief. There are people who, despite having experienced God's goodness personally, still walk away from their faith. Hebrews 6:4–6 seems to describe such a person:

> For it is impossible to restore again to repentance those who have once been enlightened, and have tasted the heavenly gift, and have shared in the Holy Spirit, and have tasted the goodness of the word of God and the powers of the age to come, and then have fallen away, since on their own they are crucifying again the Son of God and are holding him up to contempt.[1]

This passage lists several experiences such a person has with God prior to their falling away: "been enlightened," "tasted the heavenly gift," "shared in the Holy Spirit," "tasted the goodness of the word of God." This person is not doubting, wrestling with his or her faith, or questioning various aspects of God or their theology. The person described in Hebrews is also not one who has yet to experience God on a personal level. This person is not Job struggling to understand God in the midst of his pain or Thomas struggling to reconcile his theology with what others are telling him. This person described in Hebrews is one who has had the full experience, yet has rebelliously chosen to abandon his or her faith.

Faith crises do not allow us to ignore God's voice, our experiences with God, or the things that we know are right or wrong. Faith crises are not a license to sin. Although we cannot understand what goes on in the heart

---

1. NRSV.

and mind of another person, and there is no exact way to determine how a person reaches a place where they abandon their faith such as described in this Hebrews passage, there are limits to the expanse of our faith crisis journey. *However, it is important to know that God can handle our questions, our doubt, our frustrations, and our pain.* God can handle when we sin and make mistakes. God can even handle when we push God away or refuse to talk to God at various times in our lives. What *we* cannot handle is life without God, which includes taking any kind of crisis journey without God. Thomas, though doubting the experience of others, still showed up in that room with the other apostles. Job, though suffering in ways many of us will never suffer and struggling to find answers from a seemingly silent God, still directed his questions and frustrations to God.

Peter and Judas's Faith Crises

The stories of Peter and Judas during the time of Jesus' arrest provide our final biblical narratives for faith crises. Each apostle is potentially experiencing a faith crisis, and both fail in their actions of loyalty toward Jesus, but this is where their paths diverge.

As discussed in the previous chapter, the messianic paradigm, with which all of the disciples were wrestling, was not a small thing. This Jewish Messiah construct affected the Jewish people in Jesus' day and affects many Jewish people today, as some of the Jewish faith still do not accept Jesus as the Messiah. Thomas struggled with his Jewish messianic paradigm, but when he encountered the risen Lord for himself, he understood; his paradigm was changed, and he saw Jesus for who he really was. Peter and Judas also struggled with this paradigm; yet, their stories in the gospel narratives portray two different responses to faith crises: one continued to follow Jesus despite his embarrassment and failure, while the other took his own life.[2] Not much time and space is given to one of these faith crisis sojourners, while the other one continues to be prominent in the New Testament, commentaries, and books since. One became a famous leader of the church; the other became infamous, his name the very symbol of the word "traitor."

2. This work will not get into the debate of what happens to those who commit suicide and whether Christians can commit suicide and still go to heaven. Though the act of suicide is a taboo topic in the Christian community and it has not always received the understanding, empathy, and honest theological reflections it deserves, regardless of the eternal outcome of suicide, it is an action that leaves those behind with grief and sadness unparalleled by other forms of death.

Peter's Faith Crisis

In the Gospels, Peter's denial of Christ is sharply contrasted with his exuberant and passionate declaration that he would never deny Christ.[3] Dallas Willard, in his *Spirit of the Disciplines* work, connects this failure of Peter to his lack of character and spiritual development despite having been with Jesus for three years.[4] Peter, who fails miserably and publicly, reflecting cowardice that we would later see elsewhere in the New Testament,[5] stands up just forty days later, on the day of Pentecost, and delivers an effective speech calling people to a point of salvation. After Peter's public failure and his restoration by Jesus as seen in the Gospel of John chapter twenty-one, his character seems to develop enough to take the lead just over a month later, and from that moment he is seen as one of the leaders of the early church. According to Willard, it was the events that Peter experienced in the denial, post-denial, and post-resurrection of Christ that helped to shape and form his character.[6] Willard emphasizes that Peter's inner and cognitive belief in Christ was not enough at that moment of denial to prevent Peter from acting as he "normally" would with his old character.[7]

"That Your Faith May Not Fail"

In the prediction of Peter's denial, Jesus makes an interesting statement, "But I have prayed for you . . . that your faith may not fail."[8] Jesus was not praying that Peter would not deny him, but that in the denial and betrayal, Peter's faith would ultimately not fail. The prayer reflects Jesus' desire to move past the impending failure to the larger concern that Peter would not turn away from Christ after he failed. Jesus is more concerned with how this is going to affect Peter's faith than he is with whether or not Peter will commit the act itself. The guilt and shame that would affect Peter after the act would be overwhelming, as evidenced by Scripture's report that Peter ran from the scene crying. Yet, Jesus is concerned about Peter's faith in this process, not about the denial itself.

---

3. Matt 26:34; Mark 14:31.
4. Willard, *The Spirit of the Disciplines*, 72, 111.
5. See Gal 2 and Paul's confrontation with Peter's refusal to be seen with Gentiles.
6. Willard, *The Spirit of the Disciplines*, 111.
7. Ibid.
8. Luke 22:32 (NIV).

Losing Faith: The Fear and Danger

Peter, however, vehemently resists this foreshadowing by Jesus of his betrayal, saying "I will not deny you." It is as if by determination and sheer force of will alone Peter thought he could prevent himself from acting this way when the moment arrived. As Willard points out, his every intention not to fail in that moment was not enough to keep him from failing.[9] However, although Peter failed in the moment, his faith did not fail. His actions, though tied to his faith, do not completely define his faith.

Often, when discussing the story of Peter's denial, we mainly focus on Peter's denial, yet, as indicated, it does not seem to be the focus for Jesus in this passage. Moreover, the betrayal and cowardice were not the issue of the story; in fact, Jesus does not even mention it, at first. Jesus said, "But I have prayed for you, Simon, that your faith may not fail. And when you have turned back, strengthen your brothers."[10] It is only when Peter rejects such a prediction and tells Jesus that he will die with him that Jesus reveals the details surrounding the future denial. The process, the restoration, and the journey that this event will cause Peter to travel is the focus.

This life crisis of the public betrayal of Jesus did not completely remove Peter's character defect of fear. In Galatians, Paul confronts Peter over the cowardly act of avoiding being seen with Gentiles.[11] Peter had an issue with fear and insecurity, and was a coward in certain situations. Peter's natural instinct was to deny first. We know this because he did not even realize what was happening until the rooster crowed and he realized what he had done.[12] His time with Jesus had not completely changed this character defect. Peter, despite having been with Jesus for three years, cannot resist the urge in the moment to deny Jesus, which illustrates that time alone does not transform our faith and our character.

Peter had yet to experience this defining, humbling, tragic crisis of faith. Yet, it was this crisis moment that transformed Peter from the old foot-in-his-mouth Peter to the fearless proclaimer of the gospel on the day of Pentecost. Even though Peter continued to struggle with fear, he was in the process of character transformation and faith development.

---

9. Willard, *The spirit of the disciplines* : 72.
10. Luke 22:32.
11. Gal 2:11–14.
12. Luke 22:61.

"When You Have Turned Back"

The glimmer of hope in this story of failure on Peter's part is Jesus' use of the word "when": "And when you have turned back, strengthen your brothers."[13] In this narrative of predicting Peter's denial, Jesus is not giving license for Peter to deny but rather acknowledging the reality of it and hoping that when Peter acts on instinct in that moment of betrayal, Peter will remember these words of encouragement: "When you have turned back . . ." Jesus knew that the faith crisis was not going to keep Peter away eternally, and that through it, God was going to further develop Peter's character.

Judas's Faith Crisis

Not as much attention has been given to Judas by authors and commentators over the years as it is taken for granted that Judas would betray Jesus; therefore, he never really was a legitimate apostle. Samuel Laeuchli, in his discussion of Judas Iscariot, indicates that even during the time of the apostles the desire to personify Judas as the ultimate evil had begun—portraying Judas as the black sheep from the beginning of his calling as an apostle—and this desire remains today in Christian theology.[14] While there is no doubt that Judas betrayed Jesus, that he was a thief at some point as an apostle, and that Satan used him as a pawn in his evil schemes, we simply do not know enough about Judas's life or his past and can only guess as to who Judas was and why he did what he did. His actions cannot be justified and he cannot be exonerated; yet I find it hard to believe that Judas started out as Jesus' disciple *knowing* he was going to betray him.[15] The writers of the Gospels wrote from the view of hindsight, knowing that Judas betrayed Jesus; thus, from the outset of their writing, they characterized Judas as the

---

13. Luke 22:32 (NIV).

14. Laeuchli, "Origen's Interpretation of Judas Iscariot," 253–54, 256.

15. It does not seem plausible that Judas knew from the outset what he was going to do because the stage had not yet been set for the need for a betrayal and the religious leaders were not aware of Jesus at the beginning of his ministry. One of the early church fathers Origen presents a similar take on Judas, reflecting that he was not born to betray Jesus and that he did not start out planning on betraying Jesus. Origen goes deeper into the mythology of Jesus reflecting on the fact that no one suspected Judas was a betrayer or even a thief, not because he was good at hiding these tendencies, but because Judas did not enter the "apostleship" as a betrayer and thief. Ibid., 254–55.

betrayer.¹⁶ Yet, it is important to reflect on Judas prior to his betrayal in order to see him from a different perspective. If we see him as the betrayer from the start, then he has no choice but to betray Jesus. Yet, if we start from the framework that Judas's intentions from the beginning were not to betray Jesus, though he may have had serious character defects, then we can provide more reflection on how he got to the point of betrayal.

The Gospel of John provides a progression of Judas's change from apostle to betrayer in chapters 12 and 13, first identifying Judas as a thief who protested the waste of perfume that was used to anoint Jesus, then at the Last Supper indicating that by this time the devil had prompted Judas to betray Jesus. However, it is important to note that it was not until Judas took the bread from Jesus that Satan possessed him. Prior to these two events, in John chapter 6, John describes Jesus' declaration that one of the Twelve is a devil. This statement by Jesus simply reflects Jesus' knowing ahead of time that one of them would betray him. John describes the scene like this, "Then Jesus replied, 'Have I not chosen you, the Twelve? Yet one of you is a devil!' (He meant Judas, the son of Simon Iscariot, who, though one of the Twelve, was later to betray him.)"¹⁷ The declaration by Jesus does not necessarily reflect that Judas at that time had already made the decision to betray Jesus. It is possible that Jesus was describing Judas this way because of what Judas was going to do in the future, not necessarily because of who Judas was at that moment.

We know from history that during and even before the time of Jesus the Jewish people rallied around leaders who they thought might be the Messiah or might be the one to overthrow their various oppressors. We also know that one of the twelve apostles was called a "Zealot," which more than likely means that he was involved in revolutionary activity that was aimed at overthrowing the government.¹⁸ This is not to say that all of the apostles were focused on a violent or revolutionary overthrow of the Roman government; however, the Jewish messianic idea in Jesus' day was still focused on an earthly Messiah who would unite the Jewish people and take back the promised land. This Messiah would bring both spiritual and nationalistic blessings upon the Jewish people,¹⁹ yet they had no concept of the sacrificial Messiah. One who would die for the sins of all human-

16. Matt 10:4; Mark 6:3; Luke 6:16; John 6:71, 12:4.
17. John 6:70–71 (NIV).
18. Keener and InterVarsity Press, *The IVP Bible Background Commentary*, 72.
19. Niswonger, *New Testament History*, 74.

ity and usher in the spiritual kingdom of God that we do today. Historian Richard Niswonger points out that even Jesus' ministry was not consistent with what the Jewish people expected of the Messiah,[20] let alone his salvific work on the cross.

The first time we see such an understanding is Thomas' declaration in John 20; he finally understood who Jesus was. When Peter declared that Jesus was the "Christ" in Matthew 16, this was only a declaration that Jesus was the *Messiah*. The word "Christ" means anointed one and is the Greek translation of the word *Messiah*. For Peter to declare that Jesus was the Messiah only indicated that Peter believed Jesus was God's anointed leader, who was possibly going to free them from the Roman oppression but certainly would serve as king in an earthly kingdom. There is no evidence to suggest that Peter understood the deeper implication of the messiah concept, i.e., that Jesus as the Messiah came to provide a spiritual and eternal kingdom that was going to spread to the entire world. Therefore, if Peter and Thomas did not understand Jesus' divinity, there is no reason to believe that Judas believed or understood this either.

Probing questions linger regarding Judas and his faith: Is it possible that Judas, similar to the other apostles, believed Jesus to be a certain type of leader, and when Jesus started to behave contrary to his concept of the Messiah that Judas became disillusioned with Jesus and decided to sell him out? Was Judas hoping for a Jewish earthly Messiah and therefore hoping to be part of this army that would free the Jewish people from their oppressors? Questions whether Judas ever really committed to the cause of Christ are countered by whether he was any less committed than the others, who did not fully understand Jesus and what he came to do. All of the apostles abandoned him at his arrest, and Peter denied that he knew him, because they all were afraid for their lives—completely missing and misunderstanding Jesus' ultimate purpose. Furthermore, when we compare the actions of other apostles, such as James and John, who wanted to destroy people with fire for rejecting them and whose mother wanted her two sons seated next to Jesus in his *earthly* kingdom,[21] we see flawed followers of Jesus who did not understand who they were following or to what cause they had committed themselves. It is possible that Judas became jaded and upset over

---

20. Ibid., 75.
21. Luke 9:51–56; Matt 20:20–28.

what he deemed to be frivolous issues, such as a woman wasting perfume on Jesus' feet,[22] and Jesus wasting time with children.[23]

The most compelling characterization of Judas is what Judas does after the betrayal. Few people are born diabolical and sociopathic, and no sociopath feels regret for his or her actions as Judas seems to feel. Matthew reflects this experience of remorse in chapter 27:3–5:

> When Judas, who had betrayed him, saw that Jesus was condemned, he was seized with remorse and returned the thirty silver coins to the chief priests and the elders. "I have sinned," he said, "for I have betrayed innocent blood." "What is that to us?" they replied. "That's your responsibility." So Judas threw the money into the temple and left. Then he went away and hanged himself.[24]

Willem C. Van Unnik cautions against seeing in this narrative an act of repentance, as the Greek word used for our translation of "remorse" is not the same word used for "repent," but rather reflects more of a "change of mind."[25] Moreover, because we do not know the hearts and minds of people, especially from events that took place two thousand years ago, it would be impossible to assume that Judas experienced real repentance or had ever desired fully to follow Jesus. However, Matthew's Gospel does tell us that Judas and his actions are more complex than what a simple label of "traitor" suggests. Whatever his original motives, whether to help see this Jewish Messiah overthrow the government or reap financial benefit from this enterprise with Jesus, the reality is that Judas, like all of the other apostles, did not comprehend Jesus' mission. Judas, therefore, was not betraying "God," but rather a man who potentially did not meet Judas' expectations. *If Judas had understood that Jesus was God, would he have sold Jesus to the religious leaders like he did?* Although Judas does not acknowledge who Jesus was in

---

22. Matthew's Gospel positions the story of the woman anointing Jesus' feet right before Judas makes the deal to betray Jesus. Although Matthew does not identify Judas as the one who was indignant over the waste of the perfume, we know from John's Gospel that he was the one who was upset over what seemed to be a waste of money. It is possible that this was the "last straw" for Judas and was what finally prompted him to betray Jesus. Whether the impetus was the waste of money that Judas could help himself to or simply "frivolous" moments that seemed to be a waste of time, the catalyst for Judas' betrayal, according to Matthew, is this anointing event (Matt 26:6–16). The timeline in John's Gospel is compatible with Matthew, as the events all congregate within the Passover week.

23. Matt 19:13–15.

24. NIV.

25. Van Unnik, "Death of Judas in Saint Matthew's Gospel," 47.

his final act of remorse, he does not live long enough to see Jesus' death and resurrection. Judas realizes that whatever else he thought about Jesus, he was wrong to betray this man.

The purpose of this reflection of Judas is not to provide an apology for Judas's actions, but to look beyond the simplified view of his actions, in light of both Peter's and Thomas's experiences with Jesus' death and resurrection. From the perspective that all of the apostles misunderstood the messianic role of Jesus, it is possible that Judas himself experienced a kind of faith crisis—a wrestling with an outdated paradigm. This rabbi Messiah did not live up to his expectations and spent time and money on unnecessary things. Rather than continuing to follow Jesus, despite the cognitive dissonance he was experiencing, he gave in to his darker character flaws, and once the betrayal was complete, he succumbed to the guilt and shame. The ultimate question of whether Judas lost his faith, or whether he ever had faith in Christ to begin with, can never be answered here on earth.[26] That Judas gave in to temptations and his failure, however, is undeniable.

The Fight for Faith

At times, faith feels like a pressure cooker, with life applying pressure to see if we can withstand the stress and come out the other side. Dr. Charlie Self wrote a similar statement by saying, "The question for the serious follower of Christ is whether we will endure hardship for a greater reward or fall away because life is unexplainably hard."[27] Both Judas and Peter fell publicly with Jesus' arrest, but only Peter kept going, while Judas gave up. As John Maxwell made famous many years ago in *Failing Forward*, failure is not the primary concern. The primary concern is whether we fail "forward," learn from the mistake, and keep going.[28] Whether our faith is in crisis because we have failed or we are experiencing a faith crisis for situations beyond our control, and whether we continue to keep moving and growing, clinging to

---

26. The ongoing question will be whether people ever really "leave" their faith, or if their journey is all part of their faith. It seems as if it is not possible to leave one's faith, because it is part of one's belief system and worldview; however, it is possible to leave or abandon God. One's faith, therefore, more aptly described, changes and may drift away from a secure faith that understands God or that walks with God on a daily basis.

27. Self, *Flourishing Churches and Communities*, 22.

28. Maxwell, *Failing Forward: Turning Mistakes into Stepping-stones for Success*.

God through the faith crisis, are ultimately going to determine how, or if, we come out of it.

Discussing such difficult and dark topics as faith crises and the events that create crises of faith is a challenge. Although our lives are littered with challenging and difficult experiences, our human nature is to survive and overcome those challenges, or at the very least try to forget and move past those challenges. Paulo Coelho wrote this great description of our human nature: "Man struggles to survive, not to succumb."[29] There is an inherent drive within all of us to survive, move forward, fight for life, and not to succumb to the darkness that we may experience in life. After all, staying in depressing and dark moments is the very definition of chronic depression. For some people, their fight for survival is a constant use of the denial or avoidance defense mechanism, which keeps them from dealing with the dark realities of life. These defense mechanisms, though appropriate at times, if used consistently throughout life, do not allow one ever to heal. Therefore, the balance between processing and understanding those things that challenge us and not allowing the challenges and crises to overwhelm is important. We often choose simply to move beyond the challenges without dealing with or processing through them; yet, at times, the crises become too much and we cannot. The event is either too overwhelming, such as in the loss of a loved one, or our world is turned upside down by something and the foundation of our beliefs has been shaken to the core, and we simply cannot move past the crisis. It is less about choosing to deal with the crisis head-on than it is about the inability to escape the crisis that is overwhelming us. Possibly, our understanding of God and who we thought God was/is, is challenging our ability to exist and function, and dealing with it is the only way forward. Getting people to deal with or process the painful experiences in life is the very work of a psychologist and is a challenge by itself. As indicated previously, there is a larger tendency to avoid or deny challenging or painful experiences rather than deal with them head on. It is simply in our nature to avoid pain, and this is good, as it keeps us from allowing things to harm us. Yet, our aversion to pain also keeps us from dealing with the painful experiences that have affected us emotionally or spiritually, and avoiding these things can keep us from growing spiritually.

---

29. Coelho, *Veronika Decides to Die*, 8.

Losing Faith or Faith in Process?

Belief was the primary word used to describe faith of the sixty people I interviewed. As has been said, the evangelical understanding of belief has been largely equated with an affirmation or acknowledgment of a specific idea, and is used as a determining marker for salvation (a person professes belief in Jesus and thus is regarded as a Christian). Yet, one of the concerns of the focus upon such a profession or ideological view of faith is that it isolates faith from experience and understanding; a person may not be encouraged to think through or experience other aspects of faith. A person might even discount *life* experiences as *faith* experiences necessary to believe and/or trust in God. Additionally, a person may guard against any idea that may challenge one's concepts of faith for fear he or she will lose his or her faith. For example, two of the respondents who no longer professed a faith relationship with God used the phrase that they had "lost" their faith or that others in their lives were afraid that they might "lose" their faith. It is this guarding of, and resistance to, a challenge of one's conceptions of God and faith that may keep a person from experiencing a potential growth opportunity in a crisis of faith.

The interviews from my study revealed three different people whose difficult experiences had moved them away from God and into a crisis of faith, two of which were still in a faith crisis.[30] Natasha shared that she had faith in God and in people when she was younger, but in the last two years she had "lost faith in human beings." She went on to say that she feels "that God exists," but that she is not "putting effort into her relationship with God." According to Natasha, the crisis experiences have caused her to pull away from God and that her "faith is shaken,"[31] yet it is unclear whether she differentiates the experience itself from faith crises. Was it the triggering event that pulled her away from God, or was it the questioning in the crisis of faith that caused her current lack of faith in God?

The question of "cause" illustrates one of the limitations of this study and future studies. Because life is not lived in a vacuum, other contributing factors such as the challenging experience that triggers crises of faith, in addition to various responses to either the triggering event or a faith crisis, may contribute to negative results. Further development and research is needed to isolate the catalyst of crises of faith, if possible, from other factors

---

30. R122, digital recording.
31. Ibid.

to see how the internal and spiritual wrestling affects the outcome of a person's faith development. Additionally, because doubt is not widely accepted or understood in the church, and faith crises are still largely unknown or unexplored, it is unclear the extent to which the church and Christians contribute in a negative way to one's faith-crisis experience. If one does not feel the freedom to experience doubt and crises of faith, then that negativity may cause one to pull away from church or God.

Moreover, as we have discussed previously, our understanding of faith may contribute to our reluctance to struggle and doubt. Our belief in "blind" faith or the evidence of things not seen in Hebrews 11:1 implies that faith must be blind and, therefore, not based upon anything concrete or sure. The "not seen" component of our faith is the understanding that we trust in a God we cannot physical see or touch. Yet, by faith—experience, knowledge, and understanding—of who God is and what God has done in the world, we are able to come to God in faith, believing that God does exist. Faith is not formed in a vacuum without exposure to God's movement in our history or the history of others we know. Blind faith assumes no prior understanding or knowledge or experience with God, which is not possible. In order to have faith in something, we must have a prior knowledge or experience with whatever it is we have faith in. In this context, faith does not minimize knowing and understanding who God is on a larger scale. Faith is not opposed to learning, growth, and experiential understanding that leads one's faith to even deeper trust and confidence. Faith and belief in an unseen God requires enough "blind" faith without having to minimize the need for understanding this unseen God and what God has done throughout history.

The fear of losing our faith reflects a belief that our faith foundation is shaky to begin with, as if it can be easily lost; once lost, there is a fear that it will never be regained. Aaron Ross, an adjunct professor of theology at Southeastern University, referenced this concept of a shaky and tenuous faith in *Relevant* magazine. His article was in response to Michael Gungor, the Christian music artist, who questioned the literal interpretation of a six-day creation and whether Adam and Eve were, in fact, archetypes for the first humans rather than the literal first humans. The uproar that was raised over Gungor's statements sparked responses from both sides: those defending his perspective and those chastising him. In his article titled, "Why are People so Upset about What Gungor Said?" Ross made this statement:

> As Christians we tend to act like we have a belief system that is like a *bubble: It is fragile and easily popped if anything even touches any part of it.* We think we have to protect our bubble. But when did the Christian faith become so fragile? It is OK to ask the tough questions, to question our beliefs to find them to be true (and if not true to find the truth God is revealing to us).[32]

The larger issue for this book is not whether a literal six-day creation and flood took place. The broader issue is how we handle these challenges to our theology and our faith, and whether or not there are reprisals from our family, friends, and the church at large for asking such questions. Is our faith so easily lost that it cannot withstand questions to what we believe? As discussed earlier, God can handle our doubt and questions. If God can handle questions and doubt arising from tragic circumstances that question God's very goodness, can God not also handle questions regarding creation, the flood, and the exodus?

Whether or not it is possible to lose our faith may be the wrong focus. We know that we have an enemy who is roaming throughout the earth, seeking who he may devour.[33] We know that if our metaphorical house is not built well upon Jesus, when the storms of life hit, we will have nothing onto which to hold.[34] We see how all twelve of the apostles, despite having spent three years with Jesus, God in the flesh, could not grasp fully who he was, and all deserted him or betrayed him at the moment of crisis. Therefore, it is not a question of whether our faith will be shaken or whether we will experience doubts and moments of cognitive dissonance; it is a matter of when. As we saw from the beginning of this chapter in Hebrews 4, outright rebellion and rejection of God are not the same as faith crises. Jacob, Thomas, Job, and Peter's narratives reflect a genuine struggle to understand or grow. Faith must be fought for, and it can be a fight to hold on to it. Our goal must be to hang on to our faith while it is being shaken, while we are experiencing doubts, and when we want to give up. We need to focus on hanging on to our faith, not because we are afraid of losing our faith in the moments of questioning and doubt, but rather because the storms of life and the forces that are at work against us are too strong for us to go through crisis moments or faith-crisis experiences without God. So much is at work

---

32. Ross, "Why Are People So Upset about What Gungor Said?," paras. 21–22; italics added.

33. 1 Pet 5:8.

34. Matt 7:24–29.

Losing Faith: The Fear and Danger

against us that, without clinging to God, it would be easy to give in to life's pressure and succumb to the darker forces. As David wrote in the Psalms, while he was in the desert struggling for life, "My soul clings to you; your right hand upholds me."[35] Clinging to God while wrestling with our faith to the other side of the experience is what gets us through the faith-crisis experiences, rather than putting on spiritual or mental blinders that do not allow us to learn and grow from the experience. Embracing the challenge and allowing ourselves to experience the change and learn is part of the process.

---

35. Ps 63:8 (NIV).

8

Resolution of Faith Crises

A FAITH CRISIS IS a struggle between knowing one thing and coming to understand another. It is the nexus of the paradigm shift between doubt and faith and a new revelation of who God is, and the resolution of the faith crisis lies in the acceptance of the new revelation of God.

Although we hope and strive for resolutions in all aspects of our lives, as indicated throughout this work, there is a reality that life does not always provide resolutions. For example, Jacob's experience with wrestling did not necessarily result in the outcome Jacob hoped for; he still had to meet his brother Esau and deal with the consequences of his treachery. Moreover, his wrestling experience causing his hip to be wrenched from his socket and the fact that he could not overpower or manipulate this entity with whom he was wrestling would not have been a pleasant experience. The outcome that Jacob could not necessarily discern, however, was a transformation of his character. Job experienced an interaction with God that transformed his life. Peter experienced a restoration and transformation that deepened his character.

Thomas had a revelation that was the first in the New Testament regarding Jesus' dual nature as both God and man: "My Lord, and my God." No one else had quite understood or even uttered [1] this concept about Jesus until this point, and it came at the end of Thomas's struggle with doubt. His experience provides a divine statement illustrating that Jesus was both human and divine and reflects the extent to which Thomas finally understood. Thomas may have come "late to the party," but what he brought with him helped to define and understand who Jesus is.

Resolution of faith crises, as with all painful learning and growing experiences, may be different from what we hoped or desired. Our prayers are not always answered in the way that we want. The crisis event that triggers

---

1. Thomas's story is discussed in detail in chapter 6.

Resolution of Faith Crises

the faith crisis may not necessarily be resolved, similar to Jacob still having to face his brother Esau. Yet, often the resolution of faith crises are encountered through understanding God in new ways, as seen in particular with these examples of Jacob, Job, Peter, and Thomas. Therefore, it is important to note that the culmination of a faith crisis is not contingent upon the crisis being resolved, *but rather the resolution is the acceptance of a new way of viewing our faith.* This was illustrated by those interviewees whose understanding of God and/or faith changed and grew as a result of their faith crisis. *This happened even though specific answers to their questions may not have been provided, or a clear resolution to the crisis itself did not occur.* Federico Villanueva, in his discussion of the lament Psalms, indicates that "we need to be careful that we do not always enforce a theology of deliverance in all situations."[2]

Walter Brueggemann makes a similar point regarding faith and resolution in his book *The Message of the Psalms.* He says that "faith does not always resolve life."[3] This comes in his discussion of Psalm 88, the only lament Psalm that has no resolution or reframing that points back toward God. Psalm 88 starts and ends in "darkness,"[4] or, as Carlos Mandolfo says, "Like it or not, forsakenness has the last word in Psalm 88."[5] According to Brueggemann, psalms like Psalm 88 are important because

> they do not carry with them any articulated resolve of the issue. They leave us lingering in the unresolved, dangling in the depth of the pit without any explicit sign of rescue. That is an important statement to have in the repertoire, precisely because life is like that.[6]

Crisis moments may not have resolution, because life often has no resolution. The missing Malaysia Flight 370, as difficult as it is for those who have loved ones on that plane, may never be found. Resolution for those people comes not in whether the plane is found, but rather in the acceptance that it may never be found. In similar fashion, the resolution does not come as a solution to our problem, but as a change in our perspective that

---

2. Kent, Kissling, and Turner, *Reclaiming the Old Testament for Christian Preaching,* 77.

3. Brueggemann, *The Message of the Psalms,* 78.

4. Kent, Kissling, and Turner, *Reclaiming the Old Testament for Christian Preaching,* 78–79.

5. Mandolfo, "Psalm 88 and the Holocaust," 156.

6. Brueggemann, *The Message of the Psalms,* 78.

brings understanding. In the Psalms of lament and the circular movement that they illustrate there is value in the progression through the cycle, even in the challenging disorientation phase. The Psalms of lament, according to Federico Villanueva, show "that wrestling with God has value even when we fail to find the answers."[7] Therefore, as typical of many life-journeys, the value is in the journey: the wrestling, struggling, and difficult parts of the journey.

Similar to Psalm 1 and the description of the tree with its root system that goes deep into the soil in order to find the water it needs to survive, our faith root system has to deepen and stretch to find the water that is there; otherwise, the tree dies. Trees with shallow root systems cannot survive because their roots are unable to locate water. Childlike faith, therefore, is not a shallow faith. The more we experience and learn, the deeper our roots are able to go to find the water we need to survive. Job's root system before the time of testing was not shallow; had it been, Job would not have been able to survive. His roots were deep enough that he could survive the onslaught of pain and testing. Although Peter failed in the moment of trial by denying Christ, he continued to press his roots deep into the soil in the search for water. Judas, by all accounts and comparison, appears to have given up on his faith when he failed. The roots of Judas's faith appear to have been shallow; rather than press down in his faith crisis and search for the water he needed to survive, he allowed the failure to define his faith.

If we are willing to journey through the storm of faith crises, to hold onto God while our foundation shakes beneath us, our resolution will come in a deeper and more profound faith than we could imagine. Our resolution comes with a new awareness of God, a deeper faith, and an experiential understanding of God that cannot be taken away, despite the future trials we may face.

We can know God, we can understand God to the extent that we as humans are able, and we can experience God in our own theology and faith development; *this* is absolute truth. As Jesus himself revealed, he is the truth, the way, and the life.[8] Knowing vague abstractions of truth unrelated to a foundation is not faith. Knowing God through Jesus, who is truth, is the goal of faith development, and the resolution of crises of faith bring us to that point.

---

7. Kent, Kissling, and Turner, *Reclaiming the Old Testament for Christian Preaching*, 78.

8. John 14:6.

9

Understanding Faith Crises in the Church

Three Stories

Alice's Story

Alice, married with kids, served on staff at a large church, which she loved. She had been going to this church for many years when she joined the church staff. She saw ministries thrive under her leadership, and it was exciting to be where she was. Over time, however, a situation arose regarding harassment from a male member of the church. Alice rejected this person's advances and was vocal about what was happening, yet when she tried to address it with the church leadership, she was let go and the member of the church was allowed to stay. It was a devastating period in her life and a time when it seemed as if God had abandoned her. Although she had done nothing wrong and something wrong was being done to her, the drama that arose because of the situation was enough to force her to leave to keep the peace within church. For Alice, her worldview regarding church, ministry, and even God's faithfulness to her was shattered. How could God bless or have anything to do with a church that had such a corrupt way of dealing with people? How could something like this have happened to her who had served the church and God so faithfully for so many years? At the time of the writing of the dissertation, Alice was still in the middle of her faith crisis and was trying to figure out where the next steps of her life were headed.

Natasha's Story

Natasha, whom we discussed briefly in the previous chapter, grew up and was raised in the same church with her family and saw the many changes that churches inevitably go through with changing pastors and thus changing visions. Church was, for her and her family, the focal point of their lives, yet it also became a source of conflict and frustration for her and her family. Because she and her family were heavily invested and involved in their church, when she experienced hurtful interactions within that church, it plunged her into a deep and prolonged faith crisis that lasted for many years. Her faith was interwoven into her relationship with the church; therefore, when her relationship with this church was damaged, so was her relationship with God.

George's Story

George, similar to Natasha, grew up in his church and was involved in almost every part of it. Whenever the church was open, George was usually there. Raised without a father, George had a difficult home life, and he felt as if he was always struggling to fit in, both at school and church. After dealing with several medical issues and surgeries, it seemed as if what he had left of his faith was gone. He wanted to hear God's audible voice, a cry out to a God in whom he was trying to find faith, yet, that audible experience never took place, and that cemented George's belief that either God did not care, or did not exist. At the time of the interviews, George's faith in God was still almost non-existent. After a while, the church in which George grew up appeared to ostracize him, although never directly, but it showed less and less concern for his faith and well-being. When George began to rebel and exhibit questionable behavior, the church's response was largely to label him as "backslidden" and attempt to get him re-saved rather than journey with him through his time of rebellion, doubt, and challenge to his faith. Alice's crisis experience came as a result of the church, and for others like George who were in the midst of a faith crisis, the church was not a safe place to explore the crisis.

The Church

The Christian church has existed for almost two thousand years, although the concept of spiritual growth in community existed from the beginning of time. As pastor and author Bill Hybels has said, "The local church is the hope of the world."[1] However, as with any human-led entity, the church is full of human flaws. This means that if we have spent any time in church, each of us have contributed to the human imperfections within the church. Similar to our involvement in our own biological family, each person in the relational system contributes to the dynamic in both positive and negative ways. The often-used phrase regarding finding a perfect church applies: once a perfect church is found, it will no longer be perfect once one starts attending. There are no perfect churches because churches consist of imperfect people. Churches are, therefore, ultimately flawed, as we are flawed.

It is important to note before we continue that church, although never a mandatory qualification for salvation in Christianity, is important because we need each other in community and relationship.[2] The New Testament church arose out of a desire to be connected with one another after the death and resurrection of Jesus and after the mandate to be his witnesses all over the world. Just as we need each other in this frail and difficult world, so we need a local community of believers to help us, just as we help others on our faith journey. There is nothing like the sense of community and belonging that takes place when one finds a church that is healthy and committed to being that hope for the world. Yet, there is also nothing quite so painful and challenging when one is disconnected from a church, whether because one has moved and needs to find a new church or damaging and hurtful situations have caused one to leave the church.

Moreover, the church comprises a unique component in our faith crisis because sometimes the challenge to faith is related to what we have been taught or what we experience in church. With George and his faith crisis, his faith and relationship with God was directly tied to his relationship with the church. Therefore, when the issues that cause our faith crisis are tied to the church, either through theology or difficult experiences, it can become hard to separate the negative experience with the church from our faith. We know that people leave the church, at times, because of negative experiences within a specific local church. However, people also leave the

---

1. Hybels, *Courageous Leadership*, 12.

2. Pastors, and myself included over the years, in emphasizing the importance of the church, will find ways to overemphasize the role of the church in the believer's life in disingenuous ways. I have looked for Scriptures indicating church attendance is a command or mandatory, and I have failed to find any. The church is important, not because it was ever a command to be part of it, but because we as individuals need it. The question moves from whether one has to go to church to whether one should go for the health of one's life and faith.

church when they feel as if they cannot question their faith or challenge the theology within the church, as we saw with Elaine in the preface.

As discussed in chapter 1, theology is a natural result of learning and understanding more about God. Additionally, it is determining what we believe and is one of the results of the faith crisis, which is an expanded theology. Therefore, theology is simply a paradigm for understanding God. Our theology expands as a result of our faith-crisis experiences. We need to go through challenges to what we believe so that we can understand our beliefs and not simply accept those that have been taught to us or imposed upon us. Yet, the church and community of believers is not always accepting of those who challenge these accepted beliefs. By not allowing others to question, challenge, or push back against what is taught or accepted by the church, we can stunt the growth and faith development of others. Crises of faith are not always related to theology or church doctrine. Yet, when they are, the church can respond in ways that add further complications to the faith crisis rather than helping someone journey safely through it. Not allowing people to experience faith crises in a safe environment may cause them to leave the church or leave their faith altogether.

At the very core of faith crises is an assault on our theological paradigm, whether the paradigm revolves around a belief, a church, or an aspect of God. Our paradigm has been shaken, and we have to resolve the tension that is causing the foundation to shake. Yet, we simply cannot be told what the right answer is or how we should respond; we have to struggle or wrestle with our changing paradigm *because it is the process of wrestling and struggling that helps to resolve the tension or shaken foundation.* We have become very good at telling people what they should believe about any given issue; but we do not allow them to wrestle with their faith or allow them to "get there" themselves. Typically, this is where the "Christianese" or Christian platitudes come in by well-meaning Christians who offer sage advice such as, "just trust God," "all things work together for good," "we don't know why, but we just need to trust that God knows." However, such advice is already at the conclusion of the event and shuts the door on the person's need to wrestle through the emotional and spiritual struggle and come to some kind of understanding. Those of who us who offer this advice may already believe these concepts because of our own struggle and wrestling, and so we think that our experience gives us an understanding of the conclusion point the person needs to get to. What we do not realize is that this person needs to struggle to come to a conclusion on his or her own.

We can provide guidance and support, but we cannot "skip to the end" and bring people to that conclusion point without the person's own internal wrestling and struggle.

As anyone in an authority position, whether parent, teacher, or pastor can attest to, it is not always pleasant when those you are teaching or training challenge what you have taught them. Yet, we grow as individuals both when we discover concepts for ourselves and when we challenge our beliefs and understanding, to make room for ever-changing paradigms and constructs. The church also needs to realize that conflict and faith crises are normal parts of our faith journey. Challenges to our faith are more normal than they are scarce, even if people do not realize what they are experiencing.

The church needs to realize the weighty responsibility it plays in people's lives; at the same time, it needs to move beyond being seen as the only emissary of God and allow people to take responsibility for their walk with God. Allowing people to take responsibility for their faith means allowing them the space to question and doubt aspects of their faith and of what they have been taught, even by the church.

Spiritual Growth and Faith Crisis

In a study on faith development, performed at a Christian college with twelve graduating seniors, researchers discovered one of the factors that influenced or affected the seniors' faith development was the exposure to new experiences or ideas.[3] According to Elizabeth Powell, "Each participant received the new information and had to make sense of it in some form."[4] Powell went on to indicate:

> Some participants changed their belief system or had to broaden the way they saw things. Other participants shared about growth in general terms, yet all of them had to change in some way as a result of these new experiences.[5]

This study illustrates that faith development involves a system of change, particularly as it relates to exposure to new information.

---

3. Powell, "Faith Development in Graduating Christian College Seniors," 52.
4. Ibid., 53.
5. Ibid.

Powell discussed the concept of "questing," which is a "type of searching" often "characterized by experiencing new things, asking questions, and understanding new spiritual paradigms."[6] For many of the participants in Powell's study, this questing experience allowed for an acceptance of, or comfort with, doubt, whereas previously, they had been taught that it was not acceptable to question their faith or God.[7] In addition, many of the students came to the understanding that they could experience times of doubt without rejecting their faith completely, and some reported an increasing confidence in their faith due to the doubting and questioning moments.[8] Therefore, there seems to be a positive correlation between experiences of doubt, and in particular, a growth or strengthening of one's faith as a result of the doubt/crisis experience. Additionally, Powell's study underscores the role of cognitive change, as a result of exposure to new information and ways of understanding, and how this change can positively affect one's faith.

Having served in the church as a youth pastor for many of my years in pastoral ministry, I know how easy it is to reduce the concepts of Christianity to "dos and don'ts" in order to bring young people into line behaviorally. For children, "dos and don'ts" and simplified concepts of Christian theology are acceptable and needed. Yet, for young people, this is where deeper concepts of why and how must be explored, and by the time we are dealing with adults, we should move beyond "dos and don'ts" in our explanations of the Christian faith and how we interact with it on a daily basis. Helping people move beyond a "do and don't" of faith can be a challenge because often people do not want to think for themselves but would rather be told what to do and how to do it. Figuring out concepts on our own is not always something we enjoy doing. The path with the least resistance is usually what we are looking for; the mindset is, "where is the shortcut to whatever it might be, and tell me exactly how to get there."

Yet, if our simplification of the gospel message is our main way of communicating these ideas, our faith and the faith of those we lead will be shallow, thus only wading in simple ideas of a complex God. True faith grows and changes as we grow in our understanding of God, and this is faith and faith crises: a challenge to our understanding and preconceptions

---

6. Ibid., 63.
7. Ibid., 64.
8. Ibid.

of a complicated and paradoxical God who is both knowable and unknowable at the same time.[9]

Referring back to the idea of faith stages that we saw in chapter 4, which originated with James Fowler, M. Scott Peck, in *Further Along the Road Less Travelled*, developed similar faith stages, one of which is the Formal, Institutional stage. This stage reflects a more rigid and legalistic faith that conforms to the standards of behavior set by the church or church authority.[10] We find comfort and then complacency in this disciplined and conformed faith stage, and many of us stay there because it becomes easier to remain where we can simply follow directions rather than think deeply for ourselves. However, faith crises invite and then demand individual thinking and processing of one's faith and beliefs. This process is similar to how we grow as people, deciding what we think of the world and why is important to our development.

George and Natasha, whose faith crises were triggered by the church or the negative church experiences added to their faith crises, were not active in their faith or relationship with God at the time of the interview. As indicated previously, church was a significant part of their lives and intricately tied to their faith and relationship with God. For Natasha the conflict with the church and the loss of relationships that resulted from the conflict triggered the faith crisis, while for George the conflict and distancing from him that the church engaged in, added to his crisis experience. Natasha indicated that she never felt it was okay to challenge or question things, and George felt ostracized because the church deemed his behavior inappropriate and because he challenged his faith. As a result of their crises, neither individual would call themselves a "Christian" today nor reflect that they were actively pursuing their faith.

Unfortunately, Natasha and George might be seen or labeled by the church as "backsliders." The accuracy of this label is not the issue; it is our tendency to apply a label on those who leave the church, often through extenuating circumstances such as these. What if their church situations had been different and they had been allowed to grow and challenge in a

---

9. Mark 4:26–29 describes this unknowable process of how the kingdom of God grows: "Night and day, whether he sleeps or gets up, the seed sprouts and grows, though he does not know how. All by itself the soil produces grain" (NIV). The kingdom of God within us grows though we do not quite understand how it grows. Our spiritual growth correlated with the kingdom of God is not always something we can define in a ten-step process, as much as we would like.

10. Peck, *Further along the Road Less Traveled*,190.

safe place? Although conflict within any church or even relationship cannot be avoided, what if the Christian community, as a whole, and Christian theology began to recognize not only faith crises but also doubt and challenges to one's faith differently, and to allow space for people to struggle and wrestle with their faith? Similar to what we understand about child development, challenging and rebelling in healthy ways is part of the human development. Parents who are too strict with their children, never allowing them to question or challenge and "rebel" in healthy ways, can restrict their child's ability to grow in a healthy environment. Too much freedom with not enough boundaries and accountability can harm a child's development, and too many boundaries and control over a child's behavior will restrict a child's ability to mature and think for himself or herself.

The same is true for spiritual growth. When a person is in a constricted and confined spiritual environment with no room to challenge or question God, leaders, the Bible, the church, and other aspects of his or her faith, then two broad results will follow: that person might rebel against God and the church completely, or that person will stuff the questions, doubts, and challenges deep inside himself and become more like a "robot Christian" who does not feel the freedom to interact with God freely and openly.

However, one of the inherent issues with allowing people to experience faith crises is that the church is just as guilty as our society of expecting results in a microwave timeframe. We want to see people experience immediate spiritual growth and development and move past their time of struggle. Our desire to see people walk in the promises of God and become whole believers can often cause us to try and "fix" people, give them the right answers, and encourage them to do and say the right things, rather than allow them to journey through the process for themselves. The thought of seeing someone struggling with their faith for days, months, or even years may not sit well with us. However, psychologists and psychiatrists, and even medical doctors will all tell us that growth in any area of our lives does not happen overnight. (Consider the time it takes for a newborn to become a fully grown adult with both physical and cognitive adult maturity.) Physical and emotional healing and growth takes time, and so does spiritual growth.

Safe Space to Struggle

For the church and Christian theology as a whole, allowing the often disorganized and messy process that is growth to take place means also allowing

Understanding Faith Crises in the Church

space and room for all aspects of spiritual growth, which includes doubting and questioning openly without the need to provide the answers or fix that person's crisis. To borrow a concept from the late Mike Yaconelli, who was a youth pastor, then pastor for many years, spirituality is *messy*. In 2002, before his death, he came out with a book titled *Messy Spirituality*, which aptly describes our spiritual growth as well as the often misunderstood or ignored component of our faith—faith crises. He said this about spirituality:

> Accepting the reality of our broken, flawed lives is the beginning of spirituality not because the spiritual life will remove our flaws but because we *let go* of seeking perfection and, instead, seek God, the one who is present in the tangledness of our lives. Spirituality is not about being fixed; it is about God's being present in the mess of our unfixedness [sic].[11]

Faith is messy. Life is messy. Our role as sojourners on the path of faith is not to fix others, as we cannot even fix ourselves. Our role is to love, support, and guide others when needed (which is not the same as fixing the person or their problem), as they do the same for us. Our faith is not disconnected from our life because it is part of our life.

For those who are struggling in their understanding of God and how to relate to God in the midst of life's chaos and messiness, there is no three-step process. It takes time, the willingness to engage in the journey, the patience of others, and the freedom to challenge, question, doubt, and wrestle until they resolve the tension that exists. What has been reduced in Christian theology and the church to a systematized and organized category of faith development needs to become disorganized and messy once again.

The common themes of doubt and questioning our faith within faith crises illustrate that faith crises are more common than we realize, and that all of us experience some kind of cognitive and emotional discombobulating when our faith changes or grows. The stories of Jacob, Job, Thomas, Peter, and Judas have similar themes of challenges and crises, and the concepts within this work do not result in a three-step plan to resolve or avoid the crisis, but rather they are an encouragement to head into the crises, while still holding onto God and others, and, if possible, to learn, grow, and allow one's faith to expand in this painful yet necessary process.

It seems that our Christian theology needs to expand and reexamine what faith and belief really mean in light of 2,000 years of church history, which includes but is not limited to a modern understanding of a

---

11. Yaconelli, *Messy Spirituality*, 22.

systematized ordering of Christian doctrine. If understanding God from our own perspective is important, and we cannot come to a full understanding of who God is without experiencing God, then an individual's faith needs both the space and time to develop. According to Howard Stone's research on theodicy, those who counsel or minister to people in crisis should not ignore these questions, but rather provide holistic care, acknowledging that such questions are part of the "spiritual core of crises."[12] As reflected by practitioners in the field of pastoral counseling and spiritual formation,[13] this type of holistic care is happening in the spiritual formation movement that has been tied to leaders such as Dallas Willard, Richard Foster, David Benner, and Ray Anderson; however, within the church at large, holistic care is lacking and needs much more development.

Additionally, although postmodernity seems to create a culture that is more open to faith crises, there are potential dangers for those engaging faith crises. A person's questioning can lead them to a neverending spiral of doubt and deconstruction. *This is why developing an understanding of and a holistic approach to faith crises is important for both ministers and the church catholic. People need guidance and support through faith crises, and to be assured that their experiences are normal and can be beneficial in their spiritual maturity and their understanding of God.* Without the support and anchor of the church and fellow believers, faith crises experienced alone can potentially be destructive to one's faith, and this is where the church can seize the opportunities afforded by our postmodern culture to allow the space for doubt, questions, and faith crises for many people who are struggling with their faith. Faith crises can be a means to spiritual formation[14] when experienced with the support of others and the tenacious grasp upon hope.

To ignore these experiences in faith development or to encourage people to deny or suppress their questions and their doubts tends to push people further away and cause them to walk through their faith crisis alone. Denying, ignoring, or avoiding faith crises in ourselves or in others may either stunt our faith development or cause people to wander the labyrinth of questions by themselves. This is a worse danger than embracing and walking through the faith crisis with the necessary hope and wisdom.

---

12. Stone et al., "A Study of Church Members during Times of Crisis," 416.

13. Personal communication with Dani Falcioni, DMin and pastoral counselor, 2013.

14. Personal communication with Gary Black Jr., 2013.

10

Conclusion: Surviving Faith Crises

SPIRITUALITY AND FAITH ARE evolving in our postmodern world. Gone are the days when strict adherence to a set of beliefs defined a person's faith, and where church attendance and participation were a normal part of our culture. Today, Christians desire an interactive relationship with God in which they can "see" God in action in their lives, and their experiences of God help to forge their faith development. Mute and blind obedience to doctrine and/or church culture is giving way to a more individualized and experiential understanding of God, which often requires periods of developing belief. This is not necessarily nor exclusively marked by salvation experiences, but is evidence of a gradual process of spiritual formation and growth. However, experiential faith is not just a need in today's society; it is a type of faith that is reflected throughout history and seen vividly in the Bible. A crisis of faith illustrates the process of "coming to faith" that takes place in the lives of believers as their schemas change and their worldview enlarges to better understand God in a greater way.

The themes of belief and the need for experience in belief, understanding that comes through cognitive dissonance, and the role of doubt and questioning illustrate the struggle between the tangible and the intangible in our faith. Christianity accepts the reality of a God we cannot physically see, along with the reports from history of a God who took human form to redeem fallen humanity. This intangible belief yearns for a tangible experience, and this unseen reality interacts with humanity in various ways. The inherent dichotomy exists in an understanding of God as well: the God who is far beyond us is also the God who is near and never leaves us. The God who is knowable is also the God who cannot be known completely. Therefore, the Christian faith lives in the tension of paradoxically accepting things we do not understand while also striving to understand. Faith involves belief in the unseen, yet God also reveals Himself to us in various ways. We cannot see God, and though we may initially accept the intangible God, we desire a more tangible experience with this God.

There are no shortcuts to growth in our faith, nor are there ten steps to growing beyond faith crises. Even though we love neat steps and markers that indicate where we are in our spiritual journey, what we should do next cannot be reduced to simple steps. In fact, part of the faith journey and one of the things that causes faith crises is the disjointing and paradigm shifting that occurs when something takes place that was not what we planned or anticipated. Our nice, neat set of beliefs is thrown into chaos, no longer neatly organized and operating in our mind. As our foundation seems to erode, it becomes hard to process through the chaos and understand how to function once again.

However, unless worldviews grow and shift, we remain stuck in old and constricting paradigms that no longer fit our experiences. These constricting paradigms are similar to clothes that have become too small, but we stubbornly wear because we are unwilling to part with what used to "fit." Extending this metaphor to faith development and spiritual formation is crucial. If our perspective about God and our faith do not grow as we are growing, our faith will become confining, keeping us from experiencing all that God has for us. Remaining stuck in old paradigms, refusing to believe or understand new concepts regarding God and our faith, will constrict our growth, which is potentially one of the reasons some Christians do not see growth in their spiritual formation. Accepting new concepts, adapting to new paradigms, and allowing our faith to change will keep us growing spiritually.

Our faith grows when we experience God's healing, provision, or just simply God's presence in our lives. It grows when we experience a trial through which God sees us and brings us to the other side. Predictably, there will always be another challenge that is greater than the one before, and that challenge will once again cause us to rely upon our faith and understanding in God. However, as the difficulty of each crisis increases, we will experience situations where the faith we had previously is not enough. We may come to a time when it seems as if our faith no longer works, and the catch phrases and "Christianese" that brought us to where we are cannot take us past our current crisis. Our confidence level of what we can experience may be minimal compared to the insurmountable crisis before us.

For example, while reflecting upon past experiences one may wonder why he or she was so afraid or worried about a situation when it ultimately

Conclusion: Surviving Faith Crises

worked out and God brought them through. At that time, the person's faith was not enough for the moment because he or she had not experienced anything like it before. The person attempted to rely upon the faith that was built, but the fear, doubt, or worry over the situation were due to the lack of experience in such a situation. Once he or she navigated through the situation, and God brought the person through, his or her faith grew as a result. Even if the outcome was not what was hoped for, faith and confidence in God and God's ability developed on an even stronger level than before.

Once we come out of difficult situations, we know how to go through those situations in the future. We see how God provided or worked out the situation, and we know with confidence and experience that we can make it through. This, very simply put, is growth. It is how we learn and grow in all experiences in life, and the same is true for our faith. When we are exposed to a new concept or idea, the unsettling feeling or even fear of the idea continues until we come to accept (or reject) the idea and have resolved the unsettling paradigm. Eventually, we process the meaning of the idea and how it will affect our lives.

When we apply this to faith crises, a new experience or a new thought about God will cause normal tension and dissonance that will remain until we have resolved the meaning for that experience/idea. The crisis itself may or may not ever be resolved. There may be moments of wrestling with God's sovereignty, theodicy, and maybe even the church or other members of faith and their response to the crisis, but the result of the natural wrestling and processing through the faith component of the crisis can bring one to a deeper understanding of God. The understanding may simply be an acceptance that God is still good, despite the crisis, or that God still loves us, despite the tragedy that has befallen us. The understanding that emerges may be that not everything can be understood in this life because we serve a God who is beyond our ability to understand. Even in accepting that which we do not understand, it is not enough to know this about God; we have to "get there" in order to understand that which we do not understand. We have to wrestle and process so that we can understand that which we do not understand fully.

Examining the biblical narratives of Jacob, Job, Peter, Judas, and Thomas in fresh ways may help to transform our understanding of faith, doubts, and times of questioning and may work to normalize faith crises, which are often nothing more than shifts in existing ways of thinking and understanding. The story of Jacob illustrates a physical wrestling with a crisis that eventually ends up changing him internally. Jacob's story illustrates outwardly what we often feel inwardly in our own struggles. The story of Job gives us permission to question the dark moments of our lives, when what we are experiencing does not feel right or fair. The story of Peter reflects the possibility of getting up and moving beyond our crises and our failures, while the story of Judas reveals to us the danger of allowing ourselves to be swallowed up by our crisis and giving up on our faith. Lastly, the story of Thomas provides a clear glimpse of "coming to believe" and giving up old paradigms that no longer "fit." These stories do not encompass the entirety of the biblical narratives that reflect faith development and faith crisis. Yet, if we were to travel the length of the Bible, from Abraham who struggled to believe that he could bear a son in his old age, to Paul wrestling with old paradigms of who the Jewish Messiah was supposed to be and how he was supposed to act, we would see the ways in which God causes growth. The paradigms become "shaky" as something new is introduced, and in order to fit the new into the old, the paradigms have to expand or change. Adaptation allows the new to integrate with the old. These five narratives also reflect that faith crises come in all shapes and sizes: Jacob, Peter, Job, Thomas. All wrestled with their faith, all went through some type of crisis moment, and all came out the other side having learned something more about God in the process.

The extent to which we allow God to reshape our view of God is often dictated by restrictions that are self-imposed or imposed upon us by others. How the church chooses to respond to changing cultures, to changing from modernity to postmodernity, to allowing a process of growth and faith, will affect the church's ability to reach and keep people. Therefore, it would be prudent for the church to examine its understanding of growth, of faith, and of how these concepts have been, throughout Scripture, exhibited in the lives of others. Can we, in the church, allow people the space and the time to understand their faith, to grow in their faith, and to wrestle to come to their own belief? If not, the church may continue to be one source of constriction upon a person's spiritual formation and faith development.

Crises of faith deepen one's ability to trust, even though he or she may not understand fully or even agree with what God is doing. The resolutions of such faith crises are not necessarily resolutions to problems or issues that may have triggered the faith crises. Rather, the resolution is an acceptance and trust in God, who is at the core of any faith experience. Acceptance and trust do not mean a complete understanding of either God or the situation,

Conclusion: Surviving Faith Crises

but rather a faith in God that has been borne out of times of challenge and questioning, a faith that comes from a different view of God that allows one to put his or her confidence in God despite the outcome. The resolution is acceptance, confidence in God, and a fuller understanding of God, which leads to a peace that transcends all *understanding* and that guards our hearts and our minds in Christ Jesus.[1]

---

1. Phil 4:7.

APPENDIX A
Questions Used In Study

Introduction

I'm going to ask you a few questions. I want you to simply tell me what comes to your mind when you think about these concepts or events. If you don't like the terminology or wording of these questions, or if the question does not capture the way you understand or imagine the subject, please feel free to use your own wording to reframe the question to better suit your experience. I simply want your honest reflections. Do you have any questions for me?

Primary initial questions:

1. What does it mean to grow or develop spiritually?
2. How does one do that?
3. How do you understand the concept of "faith"?
4. What do you think is meant by the phrase "spiritual formation"?
5. How would you describe the development of your own faith?
6. Think about the times in your life when you have experienced significant spiritual growth. What was the situation and/or what were some of the most important catalysts that facilitated your growth?
7. Have you ever heard of the term "crisis of faith"? Yes or No. What does that term mean to you?
8. Do you perceive the crisis moments in your life to have had a positive or negative impact on the overall development of your faith? Why?
9. How did you respond to the difficult times in your life?

APPENDIX A

10. What role if any did doubt play during the difficult crisis times in your life?
11. Is there anything else you would like to add or change about what you have told me today?

APPENDIX B

Ethnographic Descriptions of Participants

Ethnicity of Participants

White/Caucasian	42
Hispanic/Latin	10
Asian	3
African American	3
East Indian	1
Middle Eastern	1

Age Range of Participants

18–20	1
20–30	11
30–40	18
40–50	13
50–60	16
60–70	0
70+	1

Education Level of Participants

High School	21
Some College	16
Bachelor's Degree	16
Graduate Degree	5
Post-Graduate	2

APPENDIX C
Additional Tables from Interviews

Faith Described as Experience
(Direct quotes are in quotation marks; researcher's questions/interactions are italicized)

Danielle	There was a moment when she "heard" Jesus speak to her, though not with her ears, but heard it from her heart
	Crying, praying at her Dad's house in the midst of the awfulness, Jesus spoke to her and told her not to worry, that she would be okay. Jesus took her tears away, couldn't even cry later on
	Because of all of her experiences, she trusts God because she knows that God has everything under control, and because God has responded to her throughout her life. She may not see what God is doing, but she trusts God.
Sandy	Been a Christian her whole life—no encounter with who God was until the point of desperation.
	"It's being absolutely confident that God is exactly who He says He is; I absolutely trust in full confidence, blindly."
	"I was so confident in my relationship with God, I loved Him, I was in conversation with Him. I was hurting so bad, that He understood, and I think he said, enough is enough, now we are going to rescue her."
	"My faith is so incredibly strong because I have seen Him over and over, prove Himself."

APPENDIX C

"I went from the first 30 years believing in God without a doubt, to, I would be an idiot if I did not believe now. I was blind and believing at first, but I would be blind and an idiot not to believe now. It switched to believing and not seeing, to how could I not believe."

Paula	Experiences started to form a belief.
	Expressed that she needs to either experience it or see it experienced in other people; has to feel it to believe it.
Joyce	"An example, someone who is going through something so terrible, trying to get out of that, feels like you are just at the bottom, feel alone, but you know you are not alone. You almost need something to happen to give you that faith or get you up again."
Francis	Seeing/experiencing miracles—helped her to trust—experienced first-hand
Evelyn	In describing how her view of God has changed, "Caricature, then Savior, now Father figure; not tangible, but an actual experience, a real character."
Ann	Now when she and her husband go through something, "God has proven himself in the past, makes it a little easier."
Christa	Growth in faith was experienced as God's presence
	The experience shook her and made her feel far from God—God showed God loved her through people, experiences, etc.
Cecilia	In describing her faith, "Believing in something not tangible, something you can't see, experiences, knowledge."
George	Audible experience with God was after all of the surgeries

Additional Tables from Interviews

Tommy	God interacted with him at various times in his life; charismatic experience; beginning of understanding about God and strongholds around 2007; 2009 experience on the mountain; directing a question to Jesus, "Why weren't you there?"
Andrew	In describing faith, "Believe in God and believe that the Bible is true—personal contact with those things-see God at work"
	Experiencing baptism in the Holy Spirit was hard, not until college—profession of faith as a child—was worried that the Holy spirit would control his mouth.
	"Have seen God do miracles-prayed for things and saw God answer."
May	"Faith isn't blind, not accepting all things just because they are said to be true—test and research faith"; God is true because she has seen the evidence of God and God's existence.
Linda	In describing her faith, "Not seeing but believing; having faith-faith in her husband that he is going to be there. Thought she had faith, but it was through the experience and the daily trust that they will do what they say."
Dorothy	She trusts in God's goodness, through personal experiences, is able to trust in God's character
Daniel	In describing faith, "it would have to involve belief as well; the belief first, or then the experience"
	"I don't think the belief is, uh, first. Because the belief comes from the experience, which I think is where the church is doing it wrong."
Cassandra	"But, um . . . we've gone through a lot of different things that just . . . multiplied it.

APPENDIX C

"You know, you learn as you go, and, one little thing that you've learned, helps to build on the next thing.

"And if he doesn't come through with what you think you need . . . um . . . it doesn't nearly matter because he knows the plans for your life."

David   "I, I, I think it's all connected. I mean I've said that I, it's something I can't see, but I, I can prove it.

Question: How?

Uh, just by these different . . . events that happened in my life, and the way that . . . um . . . really the way conflict and resolution happens. . . . spit it back out . . . the way that I understand it.

Question: So it's, it, the faith involves the visible actions, or the actions that come out of . . . ?

Yeah"

Types of Faith Crisis

(Direct quotes are in quotation marks;
my questions/interactions are italicized)

God's Existence	*Tell me about that. Did that . . . what did that do to your faith, your spiritual . . .*

"Made me, I don't think he made me . . . not believe, but . . . made me doubt."

What were some of things that . . . challenged your faith?

"I think the thing that stuck with me the most was that . . . um . . . there is, outside of the Bible there's no historical . . . historical um . . . no his, no sign of Jesus, I guess, outside of the Bible. No history about him, there's . . ."

God has always been abstract—lack of father, therefore lack of God's existence; he is a mystery; fooled himself at times

Additional Tables from Interviews

	or make himself believe that God is real. Doesn't believe God exists.
Theology	Winter season, night time of our discontent, heightened experience—a lot of winters and cold spells—not necessarily many crises experiences—spiritual crisis is over—intellectualism and going through a spiritual crisis presently.
	"Leaving [name of church] I think was deep and the depth of where I felt, and could call it that . . . a crisis of faith."
	So, if I could say . . . your faith development . . . has been more at odds with the theology or the doctrine . . .
	"Exactly."
	. . . of religion.
	"Exactly."
	Than it has been with either God or the Bible.
	"No, no . . . yeah, yes, exactly. It's not the Bible . . ."
	[Son] was prayed for/deliverance ministry, but nothing really changed.
	He wondered if the biblical model of Christian family failed.
	"Life wasn't supposed to be that way."
	"Critical awareness that what I have believed up to a point does not work anymore"; paradigms shift; understanding of faith in God, God's kingdom, and my role in God's kingdom changes, paradigms no longer work. "The crisis comes in when we question everything."
	"Yes—a point where something you have believed makes you question or wonder if what you believed is really true."
	"Or maybe it sort of could cause you a lack of belief, or doubt, or anger in God, where . . . you know, maybe you could sort of rebel against . . . or what have you."

APPENDIX C

Faith | Question your faith; challenge, go to a place where you had to realize, do I believe or do I not. I have been there and experienced that crisis of faith.

When something happens in your life that calls into question what you believe, shakes your faith—that experience of moral failure was her crisis of faith—had to understand that God still loved her—the experience shook her and made her feel far from God—God showed God loved her through people, experiences, etc.

Began to question everything she learned as a child—attached her faith to her parents' truth and not necessarily the gospel truth, so she had to separate what her parents believed from what she believed. We can have a relationship with interaction with Christ daily.

Or a crisis that means you doubt your faith—(this is what happened to her)

Personal crises. I mean, you start to, you start to question things because it if that person can fall, that person is who he says he is, if they can attain that maturity, so they fall, it starts to make you question, backtrack all the way back to question everything out. . . .

Well, it was like a healing cuz I had gone into a deep depression and um . . . just a nervous breakdown. I, I was, just could hardly put two sentences together for a while there, and that was . . .

Did anything precipitate it or was just kind of an out of the blue . . . ?

It was . . . a combination of many things. It was a combination of me . . . challenging my faith . . .

I don't think I would call it a crisis, I think most of the time my faith has been there. *Rephrased to emphasize "changing" the way you see your faith?* Yes, definitely.

Additional Tables from Interviews

Belief(s) about God	"At some point, I would ask people, what should I do, and now I am stuck with this person for the rest of my life because he was her daughter's Dad. For a few weeks I was immobile, and I didn't want to do anything. Okay, God, what am I going to do. That was the first time I felt like (him) and as if he patted me on the shoulder and said, it's okay, everything's going to be okay."
	Did it feel as if it opened a new chapter in your relationship with God?
	"Yeah, it just changed my perspective on God."
	Wasn't allowed to question God; get angry, depressed
	Hasn't allowed her to grow
	No personal connection—
	Feel guilty

Questions/Questioning Experience

Yvonne	Did not understand why she felt this way
	She and her spouse were in youth ministry, "therefore this shouldn't be happening to her—this isn't me, why am I being punished?"
	"If I can't function as a human being, why is God keeping me here?"
	"Why can't God just teach me in an easier way?"
Danielle	Last incident with her son-instead of asking "why," "now it is thank you for bringing this to my attention so that he can get help."
	(Previous experience) Came home at one point during daughter's medical crisis, cried out to God, crying, screaming, "where are you"?

APPENDIX C

Sandy	Angry at God—why would you allow this to happen?

Question your faith; challenge, go to a place where you had to realize, do I believe or do I not?

"I was angry at God because of my marriage." To God, "How could you let me marry someone like this?" "When you get disappointed by God, that really leads you down a dark path; "you know He's real, but He's not acting on your behalf." At the root of it, was hurt at God that He would allow me to go down this path—never verbalized this before—it was my disappointment with God.

Paula	Her growth has always been "up and down," with "huge questions"

"Is God even real? How do I know that? He doesn't talk to me, how do I know? When anything major happens in my life, I always question it: what's the purpose, why do I need to go through that?"

"Doubt to me means questioning. It's my way of working through the situation or the issue. Doubt is a positive, because if you don't question anything, then you are just blind. Doubt is a good thing."

Ethan	"God where are you, do you still love me?"
Joyce	"... but when you lose somebody, like I lost my grandma, it's like why? You almost want to hate God for it; like why?"

Do you feel like you have resolved those questions of why?

"You never really get an answer for the why."

"If you love me then why I am going through all of this?"

It's the question of "why" again.

"Yeah, it's always why. A lot of times you are never going to get an answer for your why"

Additional Tables from Interviews

Isabella	The crisis comes in when we question everything.
	Felt like she couldn't trust God; then her brother could not find work; "what's so hard God about giving my brother a job"; heart breaks because her brother and family struggle with finances; "why is God not doing it?"
Christa	Faith journey became less about knowing everything and more about knowing nothing—began to question what was important, the rules, how we are taught to understand the roles—everything turned on its head
Cindy	Met with priest for 6 weeks bringing her questions/issues about her Catholicism—when she met with him the first time, on the cusp of being gone forever
	Would faith be as solid if she had not questioned?
	No. Many Catholic's faith is not deep because they don't question.
Natasha	"Wasn't allowed to question God; "get angry, [and] feel guilty"
	Family does not allow her to question the [name of church] doesn't allow her to question at all.
Cecilia	Question what she believed and why she believed what she did; didn't feel God was with her
Elana	Brother died, doubted, angry, rejected God; didn't understand how God could do that
George	God was distant and the church was misleading; arrogant and wouldn't allow itself to be challenged (questioned)
Andrew	[Son] was prayed for/deliverance ministry, but nothing really changed. He wondered if the biblical model of Christian family failed. Life wasn't supposed to be that way.

APPENDIX C

Fran	Moments where she doubted God would answer—"what's the point?"
Lisa	Brother died—God had abandoned her; back to asking why, why God; "wished I knew if God understands my pain-question is still there today"; "why is she [mom] still here"; major medical issues after her brother died; doesn't even ask God to take her anymore; "wonder if prayer makes a difference"; "how can I trust you with this, you have your own agenda, God"
Stacy	Questioned God—didn't feel the freedom to question God until the last decade
Samuel	Time when he and his wife were having trouble—talked with their pastor; he indicated, "I've done all the right things," why is this happening?
Abriella	Doubt that God knew what God was doing, that this is what God's plan for her life was
John	All these things caused him to question where God was in all of that
	How did you resolve the where is God question?
	Realized he needed to re-focus on God, girlfriend had become too important to him
René	"Wonder if we don't question our faith, faith becomes stagnant or not real" Faith was not real to her until last year; come to a point where you question and figure it out for yourself
	What was the questioning process like?
	Believed with head but not heart
	What triggered questioning?

Additional Tables from Interviews

	Experience faith on a different level or a different context—didn't need faith to sustain me.
	Began to question everything she learned as a child—attached her faith to her parents' truth and not necessarily the gospel truth,
Linda	"How can people do this to me again?"
	Doubting who they were—doubted if she could trust church people again—learn,
Ruth	"If my faith is as strong as it is, I shouldn't be this depressed, should be able to overcome this." Doubted her faith; the questions helped somewhat
	Questions kept coming up, but she wanted to know the truth-kept coming back to what she knew
Juanita	Doubted everything she had been taught-everything has to be true
	Mormonism was her life, everything; always had questions, when sick began to question (patriarchal blessing) the only reason she was sick was because she was sinning and doing something wrong; then went through a time of repentance.
Daniel	"Doubt comes around a lot; Am I Just making this up in my head? Is God really real? Wrestle with faith issue; "God are you there?"
	Do you feel comfortable to doubt?
	"Yes, doubt causes us to doubt and dig—two d's, when I start doubting, I start digging—the depth of the valley determines the height of the mountain."
Allan	"As the older I got, the more I was to question things, is it coincidence, was it God"
Tommy	"[God] Why weren't you there?"

APPENDIX C

Elton	Started to question if there was something bigger than God or the pain

Those who Expressed No Doubt Experience

Note: Because doubt tends to be used synonymously with questioning our faith, I combined the use of doubt with the concept of questioning, when appropriate, and in one situation, with a faith crisis.

Julie	No doubt, even when she was going through everything she went through,
Francis	Never experienced moments of doubt or losing faith
Anne	"I doubt myself more than I doubt God. If I feel like God is not coming through, then I think maybe I am wrong, or missed something, I doubt whether my issue is big enough or important"
May	No experiences of anger, frustration, or doubt about God—never experiences that, sees it as arrogant
Lisa	Not necessarily doubt, but wondering if trial is because of her being Christ spiritually—but she doesn't believe that God took her brother because of her spirituality.
Philip	More profound doubt about himself than about God; doubting his ability and concern over whether he would fail. Doubt about ministry and his effectiveness—moved from institutional-style of religion to more of a home church
Sophia	*Have there been other forms of doubt, not related to God's existence, but related to God . . . Have there been other doubting experiences other than doubting the existence of God, times of doubt . . . you and God?*
	"I don't think so . . ."

Additional Tables from Interviews

Sharon "... when I was younger in my faith ... younger in my walk, and less experienced with life; there was a lot more doubt. I don't really doubt ... um ... faith or God or any of that; that, those aren't my doubts. No, I still, I still tend to get disappointed in humans and human nature, and I get disappointed in my circumstances. ...

... but I don't doubt my faith."

Bibliography

Adams, Daniel J. "Toward a Theological Understanding of Postmodernism." *Cross Currents* 47 (1998) 518–30.

Armstrong, Karen. *A History of God : The 4000-Year Quest of Judaism, Christianity, and Islam*. 1st American ed. New York: Knopf, 1993.

Armstrong, Terry R. "Revisiting the Johari Window: Improving Communications through Self-Disclosure and Feedback." *Human Development* 27, no. 2 (2006) 10–14.

Black, Gary, Jr. *The Theology of Dallas Willard: Discovering Protoevanagelical Faith*. Eugene, OR: Pickwick, 2013.

Briggs, David. "Forgiveness in Its Own Time: How Faith Communities Can Help Trauma Survivors Heal." In *The Press Room*, 2014. http://blogs.thearda.com/trend/featured/forgiveness-in-its-own-time-how-faith-communities-can-help-trauma-survivors-heal/ (accessed October 28, 2014).

Brueggemann, Walter. *The Message of the Psalms : A Theological Commentary*. Augsburg Old Testament Studies. Minneapolis: Augsburg, 1984.

Calvin, Jean. *Commentaries on the Epistles of Paul to the Galatians and Ephesians / by John Calvin*. Translated by William Pringle. Grand Rapids: Eerdmans, 1948.

Coelho, Paulo. *Veronika Decides to Die*. 1st U.S. ed. New York: HarperCollins, 1999.

Fowler, James W. *Faithful Change: The Personal and Public Challenges of Postmodern Life*. Nashville: Abingdon, 1996.

———. *Stages of Faith : The Psychology of Human Development and the Quest for Meaning*. 1st ed. San Francisco: Harper & Row, 1981.

Frohlich, Mary. "Spiritual Discipline, Discipline of Spirituality: Revisiting Questions of Definition and Method." *Spiritus: A Journal of Christian Spirituality* 1, no. 1 (2001) 65–78.

González, Justo L. *The Reformation to the Present Day*. Vol. 2 of *The Story of Christianity*. 1st ed. San Francisco: Harper & Row, 1984.

Grenz, Stanley J. *A Primer on Postmodernism*. Kindle book. Grand Rapids: Eerdmans, 1996.

Habermas, Ronald T. "Doubt Is Not a Four Letter Word." *Religious Education* 84, no. 3 (1989) 8, 402–10.

Harstine, Stan. "Un-Doubting Thomas: Recognition Scenes in the Ancient World." *Perspectives in Religious Studies* 33, no. 4 (2006) 435–47.

Hartley, John E. *Genesis*. New International Biblical Commentary Old Testament. Peabody, MA: Hendrickson, 2000.

Bibliography

Holcomb, Gay L., and Arthur J. Nonneman. "Faithful Change: Exploring and Assessing Faith Development in Christian Liberal Arts Undergraduates." *New Directions for Institutional Research* 122 (2004) 93–103.

Hunsberger, Bruce, et al. "Religious Fundamentalism and Religious Doubts: Content, Connections, and Complexity of Thinking." *International Journal for the Psychology of Religion* 6, no. 3 (1996) 201–20.

Hybels, Bill. *Courageous Leadership*. Grand Rapids: Zondervan, 2002.

Keener, Craig S., and InterVarsity Press. *The Ivp Bible Background Commentary: New Testament*. Downers Grove, IL: InterVarsity, 1993.

Kent, Grenville J. R., Paul J. Kissling, and Laurence A. Turner. *Reclaiming the Old Testament for Christian Preaching*. Downers Grove, IL: IVP Academic, 2010.

Krause, Neal. "Religious Doubt and Psychological Well-Being: A Longitudinal Investigation." *Review of Religious Research* 50 (2006) 287–302.

Krause, Neal, and Keith M Wulff. "Religious Doubt and Health: Exploring the Potential Dark Side of Religion." *Sociology of Religion* 65, no. 1 (2004) 35–56.

Laeuchli, Samuel. "Origen's Interpretation of Judas Iscariot." *Church History* 22, no. 4 (1953) 253–68.

Lewis, C. S. *The Complete C.S. Lewis Signature Classics*. 1st ed. San Francisco: HarperSanFrancisco, 2002.

Livingston, James C. *Anatomy of the Sacred: An Introduction to Religion*. 6th ed. Upper Saddle River, NJ: Prentice-Hall, 2009.

Maas, Robin, and Gabriel O'Donnell. *Spiritual Traditions for the Contemporary Church*. Nashville: Abingdon, 1990.

Mandolfo, Carleen. "Psalm 88 and the Holocaust: Lament in Search of a Divine Response." *Biblical Interpretation* 15, no. 2 (2007) 151–70.

Maxwell, John C. *Failing Forward: Turning Mistakes into Stepping-Stones for Success*. Nashville: Nelson, 2000.

May, Gerald G. *The Dark Night of the Soul: A Psychiatrist Explores the Connection between Darkness and Spiritual Growth*. 1st ed. San Francisco: HarperSanFrancisco, 2004.

McGrath, Alister E. *Christian Spirituality*. Malden, MA: Blackwell, 1999.

Mursell, Gordon. *The Story of Christian Spirituality: Two Thousand Years, from East to West*. 1st Fortress Press ed. Minneapolis: Fortress, 2001.

Myers, Allen C. *The Eerdmans Bible Dictionary*. Grand Rapids: Eerdmans, 1987.

Newman, Barclay M., Jr. *A Concise Greek-English Dictionary of the New Testament*. Stuttgart, Germany: German Bible Society, 1993.

Niswonger, Richard L. *New Testament History*. Grand Rapids: Academie, 1988.

O'Brien, J. Randall. "World, Winds, and Whirlwinds: The Voice of God Meets 'the Vice of God.'" *Perspectives in Religious Studies* 30, no. 2 (2003) 151–60.

O'Brien, Kelli S. "Written That You May Believe: John 20 and Narrative Rhetoric." *Catholic Biblical Quarterly* 67, no. 2 (2005) 284–302.

Peck, M. Scott. *Further along the Road Less Traveled: The Unending Journey toward Spiritual Growth: The Edited Lectures*. New York: Simon & Schuster, 1993.

Peloso, Jeanne. "The Theological Anthropology of Young Adult Catholics in Postmodern America." *Pastoral Psychology* 61, no. 2 (2012) 233–43.

Penner, Myron B. *Christianity and the Postmodern Turn: Six Views*. Grand Rapids: Brazos, 2005.

Powell, Elizabeth S. "Faith Development in Graduating Christian College Seniors: A Qualitative Study." PsyD diss., Azusa Pacific University, 2010.

Bibliography

Puffer, Keith A., et al. "Religious Doubt and Identity Formation: Salient Predictors of Adolescent Religious Doubt." *Journal of Psychology & Theology* 36, no. 4 (2008) 270–84.

Ricœur, Paul. *The Symbolism of Evil*. 1st ed. Religious Perspectives. New York: Harper & Row, 1967.

Ross, Aaron. "Why Are People So Upset About What Gungor Said?" *Relevant*, August 8, 2014, http://www.relevantmagazine.com/current/why-are-people-so-upset-about-what-gungor-said#dUDcAuj6aUf59V3p.99 (accessed August 8, 2014).

Self, Charlie. *Flourishing Churches and Communities: A Pentecostal Primer on Faith, Work, and Economics for Spirit-Empowered Discipleship*. Grand Rapids: Christian's Library, 2013.

Stone, Howard W., et al. "A Study of Church Members During Times of Crisis." *Pastoral Psychology* 52, no. 5 (2004) 405–21.

Tite, Philip L. "On the Necessity of Crisis: A Reflection on Pedagogical Conflict and the Academic Study of Religion." *Teaching Theology & Religion* 6, no. 2 (2003) 76–84.

Van Unnik, Willem Cornelis. "Death of Judas in Saint Matthew's Gospel." *Anglican Theological Review* 3 (1974) 44–57.

Willard, Dallas. *The Spirit of the Disciplines: Understanding How God Changes Lives*. San Francisco: HarperSanFrancisco, 1990.

Yaconelli, Mike. *Messy Spirituality: God's Annoying Love for Imperfect People*. Grand Rapids: Zondervan, 2002.

Subject Index

Abraham, 23–24, 64, 114
Bacon, Francis, 11
Black Plague, The, 17
Calvin, John, 11–14, 24
Cognitive Dissonance, 9, 35, 37, 41–48, 52–53, 56, 92, 96, 111
Dark Night of the Soul, 36–37
Enchanted, Movie, 45
Enlightenment, The, 11, 17, 20
Faith Development Theory, 49
Gungor, The Michael Gungor band, 95–96
Hezekiah, King of Judah, 66–67
Jacob, 9, 42–44, 96, 98–99, 109, 113–114
Job, 4, 9, 61–68, 84–85, 96, 98–100, 109, 113–114
Johari Window, 16n15
John, the Apostle, 30, 79–81, 89–90
Judas Iscariot, 9, 79, 85, 88–92, 100, 109, 113–114
Luther, Martin, 11–14
Malaysia Flight 370, 59n9, 99
Matrix, The, Movie, 2
Modernity, 11–12, 16–17, 20, 114
Moses, 64n27

Orthodoxy, 14, 16, 33–34
Orthonous, 33–34, 69
Orthopraxy, 33
Paul, the Apostle, 3, 15, 23–24, 86–87, 114
Peter, the Apostle, 9, 79–81, 85–88, 90, 92, 96, 98–100, 109, 113–114
Postmodernity, 16–21, 34, 75, 110, 114
Premodernity, 11–12, 17
Protestant Reformation, The, 12
Red Sea, The, 31–32n45
Ricoeur, Paul, 51–53
    Critical Distance, 51–53
    First Naiveté, 51, 53
    Second Naiveté, 51, 53
Stages of Faith, see Faith Development Theory
St. John of the Cross, 36
Systematic Theology, 11–13, 15–16, 19–20, 34
Teresa of Avila, 14, 36
Thomas, the Apostle, 9, 29, 70, 78–85, 90, 92, 96, 98–99, 109, 113–114
Wesley, John, 1, 14

Author Index

Black, Jr., Gary, xi, 30, 35, 49
Brueggemann, Walter, 52–53, 99
Calvin, John, 24
Coelho, Paul, 93
Fowler, James, 28, 31, 45, 49–51, 53–54, 107
Gonzalez, Justo, 13–14
Grenz, Stanley, 11, 13, 17–18
Habermas, Ronald, 71–72, 77
Hybels, Bill, 102
Lewis, C. S., 54, 67–70
Livingston, James, 27–28, 31, 60
Maxwell, John, 92
Peck, M. Scott, 107
Ross, Aaron, 95
Willard, Dallas, 14–15, 28, 34–35, 86–87, 110
Yaconelli, Mike, 109

www.ingramcontent.com/pod-product-compliance
Lightning Source LLC
Chambersburg PA
CBHW070910160426
43193CB00011B/1420